BERKLEE PRESS

CONTEMPORARY JAZZ GUITAR SOLOS

T0071278

MICHAEL KAPLAN

BERKLEE PRESS

Editor in Chief: Jonathan Feist
Senior Vice President of Online Learning and Continuing Education/CEO of Berklee Online: Debbie Cavalier
Assistant Vice President of Marketing and Recruitment for Berklee Media: Mike King
Dean of Continuing Education: Carin Nuernberg
Editorial Assistants: Emily Jones and Eloise Kelsey
Cover by Small Mammoth Design

ISBN 978-0-87639-165-5

DISTRIBUTED BY

online.berklee.edu

1140 Boylston Street
Boston, MA 02215-3693 USA
(617) 747-2146

Visit Berklee Press Online at
www.berkleepress.com

HAL•LEONARD®
CORPORATION
7777 W. BLUEMOUND RD. P.O. BOX 13819
MILWAUKEE, WISCONSIN 53213

Visit Hal Leonard Online
www.halleonard.com

Berklee Press, a publishing activity of Berklee College of Music, is a not-for-profit educational publisher.
Available proceeds from the sales of our products are contributed to the scholarship funds of the college.

CONTENTS

INTRODUCTION

I am honored to have written this second book of jazz guitar transcriptions, following the positive reception of my first book, *Bebop Guitar Solos* (Berklee Press, 2014). While working on this new volume, I came to fully appreciate the jazz lineage and how the music has developed over the years. The difference is profound between the more traditional players in the bebop book, such as Wes Montgomery and Joe Pass, and the more modern players discussed in this volume, such as John Scofield and Mike Stern. It truly shows how the language of jazz has progressed and grown over time.

The syntax of the language and the melodies, harmonies, and technique on the instrument have become more and more complex, over the years. The contemporary language of jazz now contains elements that it did not in the past. Many more influences can be heard in the music as compared with the decades before. These include, but are not limited to, influences of rock, pop, funk, R&B, and even music from different cultures around the world.

That being said, you will see some examples of phrases in this book that are not significantly different from those of the classic bebop players. This is because the majority of modern musicians have a firm understanding of the players who came before them, and use that knowledge to develop their own style and propel the language forward. We all know the stories of Wes Montgomery figuring out Charlie Christian solos, George Benson and Pat Metheny figuring out Wes Montgomery solos, and so on. They, of course, put their own personality into those phrases, add things in, take things out, and the language naturally changes. No one knows what the future holds, and the only thing that is constant is change. Like most languages, jazz will keep evolving and will never stop.

These solos were transcribed from some of the most influential modern jazz guitarists. The original recording is noted in the section about each tune, and it is imperative to listen to the recordings of the transcriptions before playing them. I strongly suggest being able to first sing—or at minimum, hear the solo in your head—before playing it. By doing so, you'll accomplish a quicker assimilation from the notes on the pages to your guitar.

The tablature provided for each solo is a suggestion, instead of a "must be played this way" directive. There are many different ways to play the same phrase on the instrument, and ultimately, that decision is for you to make. Regardless of what position and fingering you decide to use, it is my belief that you need to "see" the chord and scale underlying each phrase. That being said, I propose that you start with the string choices shown in the tablature. If a fingering does not suit you, search for an alternative. After all, this is jazz, and everyone comes at it from his or her own perspective. All of the jazz guitarists who created these solos are jazz guitarists, but they all play differently and approach fingering from their own angle.

There is no recommended order to these transcriptions; start wherever you choose. If you listen to a solo, it moves you, and you feel inspired by it, then go ahead and begin learning that one. If along the way, you find that you like a specific guitarist's playing, I encourage you to seek out more recordings by that artist, and dig deeper into their specific style of improvisation. Many times, you will find that a musician has a certain method to their playing that is quite consistent and predictable. In addition, I suggest practicing any phrases that you like in all keys.

Happy playing!

1. JIM HALL

"Billie's Bounce"

"Billie's Bounce" is from the Jim Hall album *Live in Tokyo*. The album was recorded live at the Nakano Sun Plaza Hall in Tokyo, Japan, on October 28, 1976. It features Don Thompson on bass and Terry Clarke on drums.

Jim Hall is certainly a more classic than modern player. However, he is included in this book because many modern guitarists consider him to be the father of modern jazz guitar and look to him for inspiration. Although it was very difficult to choose only a few phrases to discuss from this incredible solo, I decided to focus on some similarities in how Jim negotiates his way through measures 8–9 of the blues form: the III VI chord progression resolving to a II chord. These are examples of classic ways to play over a II V chord progression. However, similar ideas can be found in most modern guitarists' playing as well. Notice how he hits the F♯ every time over the D7 chords.

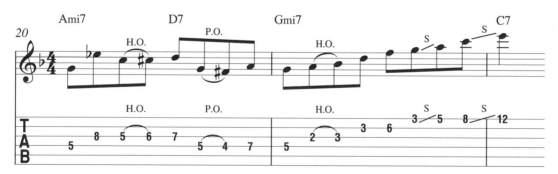

FIG. 1.1. "Billie's Bounce" Measures 20–22

FIG. 1.2. "Billie's Bounce" Measures 44–45

FIG. 1.3. "Billie's Bounce" Measures 56–57

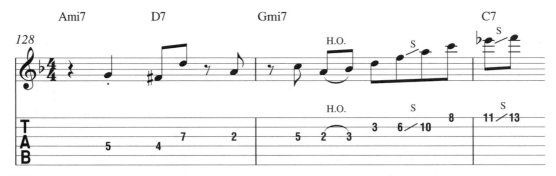

FIG. 1.4. "Billie's Bounce" Measures 128–130

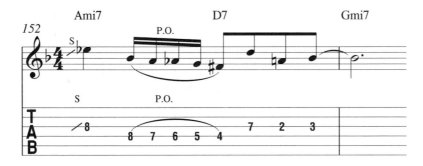

FIG. 1.5. "Billie's Bounce" Measures 152–153

Billie's Bounce
(Bill's Bounce)
Solo by Jim Hall

By Charlie Parker

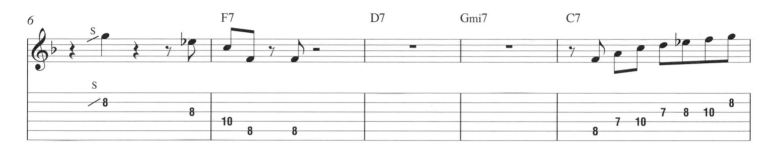

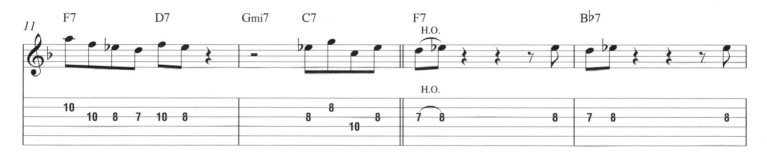

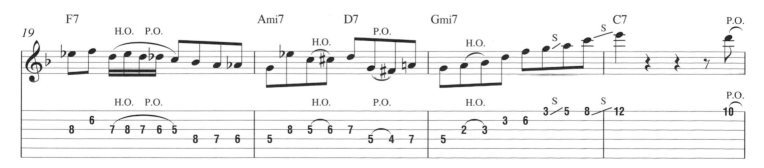

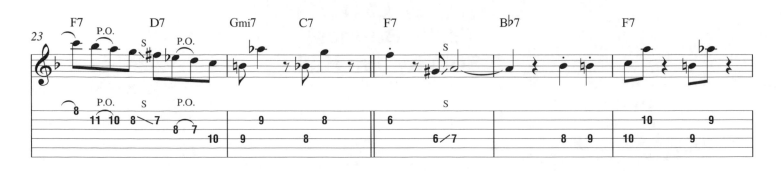

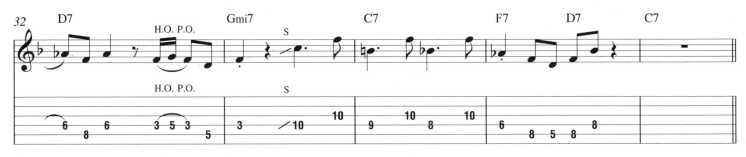

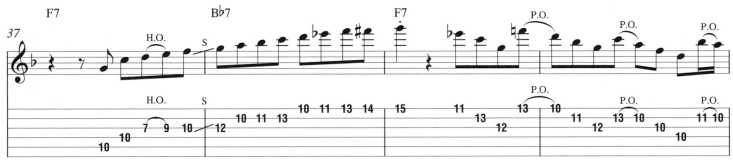

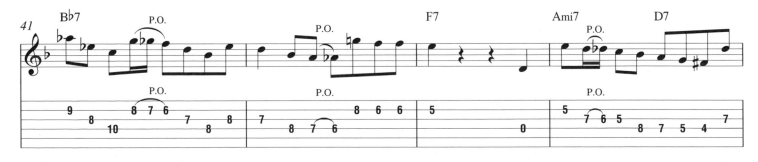

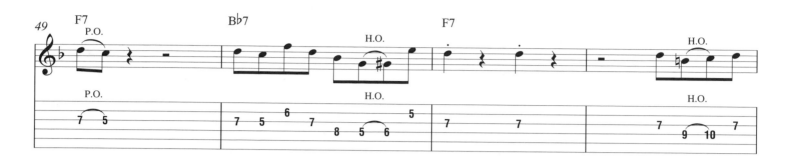

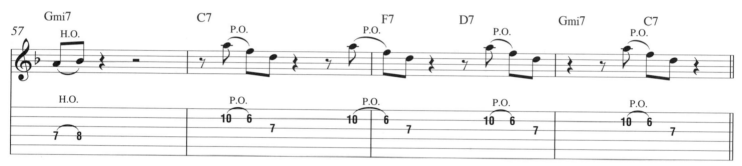

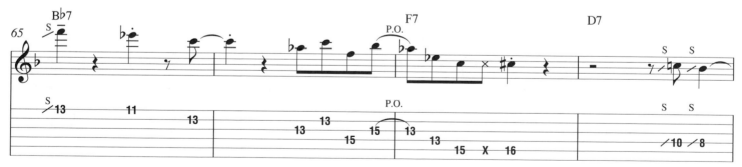

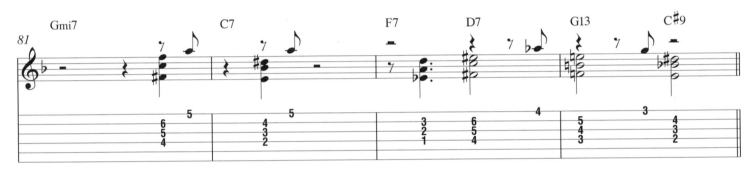

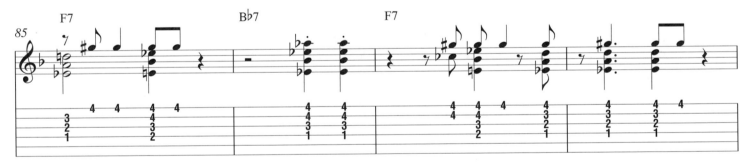

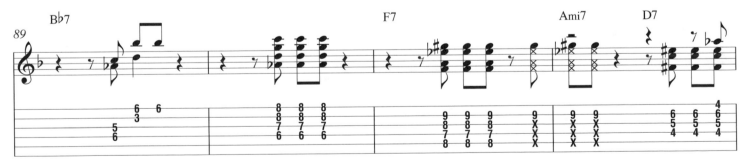

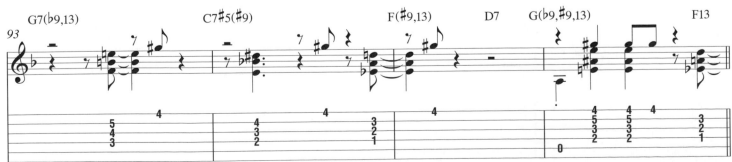

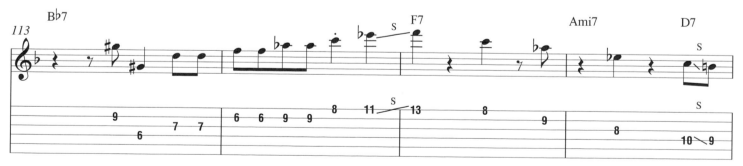

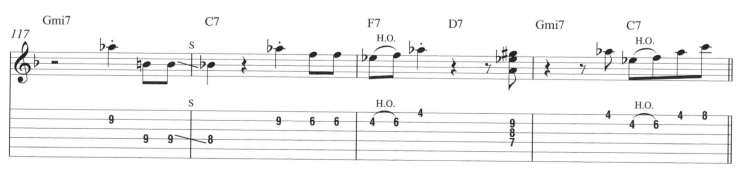

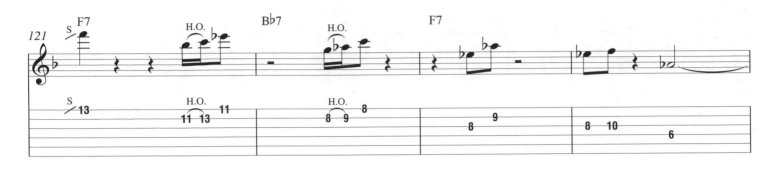

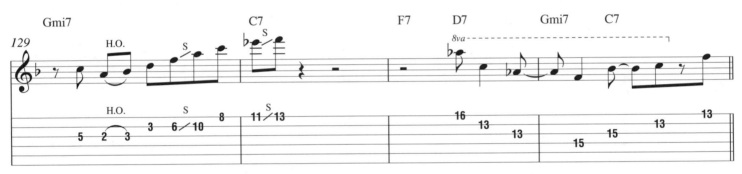

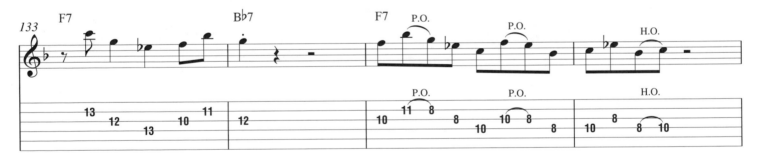

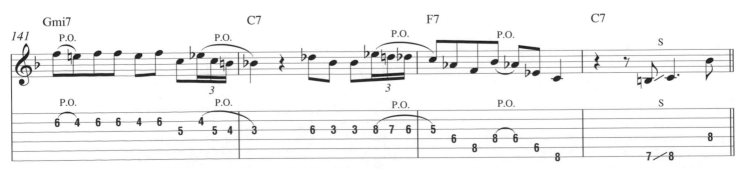

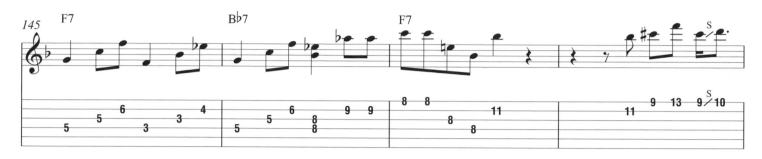

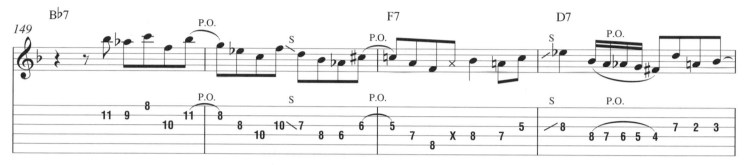

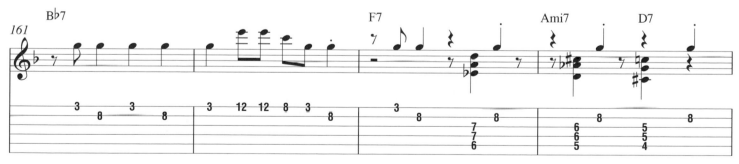

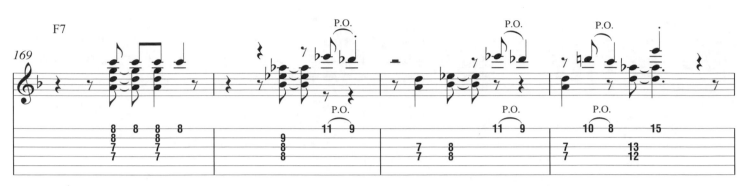

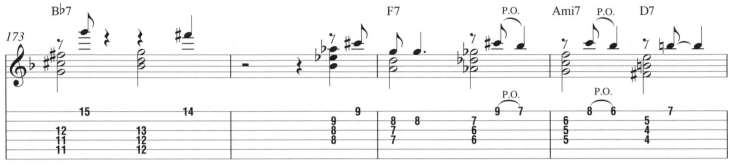

FIG. 1.6. "Billie's Bounce"

2. JIM HALL

"St. Thomas"

"St. Thomas" is also on Jim Hall's album *Live in Tokyo*. Note how Jim plays over the III VI II V progression in measures 10–13 of the sixteen-bar form of "St. Thomas" (see figures 2.1 and 2.2). He plays very simply, showing that with both classic and more modern jazz, you do not need to play complex rhythms and harmonies. With the exception of outlining the A7 chord in the second measure of each phrase by playing a C♯, he plays scalar and diatonically in the key of C major.

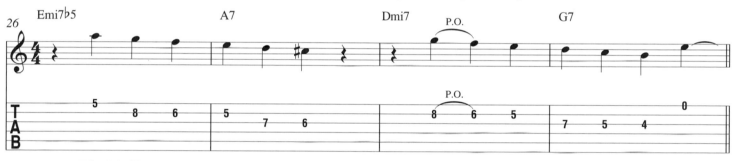

FIG. 2.1. "St. Thomas" Measures 26–29

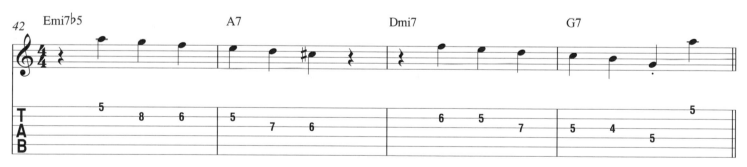

FIG. 2.2. "St. Thomas" Measures 42–45

Measures 58–61 sound a little more modern because of the rhythmic motif used by Jim. He uses this rhythmic motif to slide into the chord tones of the 3rd (C♯) of the A7 chord in measure 59, the root of the D minor 7 chord in measure 60, and again the 3 of the G7 chord (B) in measure 61.

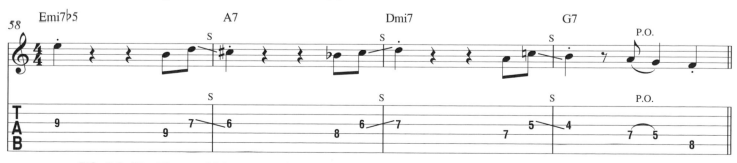

FIG. 2.3. "St. Thomas" Measures 58–61

St. Thomas
Solo by Jim Hall

By Sonny Rollins

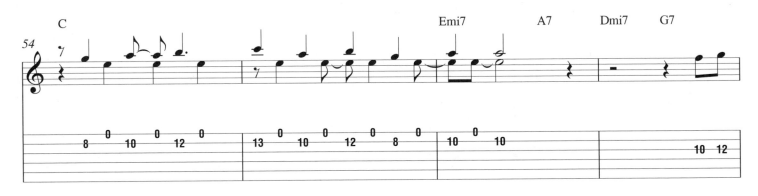

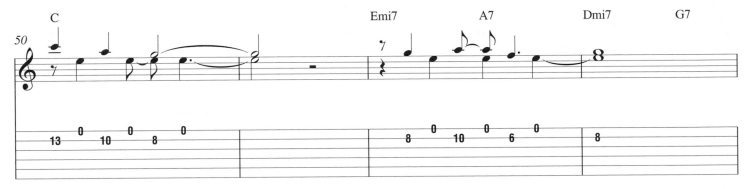

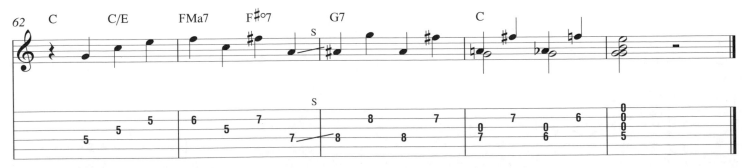

FIG. 2.4. "St. Thomas"

3. JOHN SCOFIELD

"If I Were a Bell"

"If I Were a Bell" is from the Gary Burton and Friends album *Departure*. It was recorded on September 20–22, 1996 and released in 1997. The lineup included Gary Burton on vibraphone, Peter Erskine on drums, Fred Hersch on piano, and John Patitucci on bass.

Measures 17–18 are an example of John playing somewhat "outside." Although I look at it as a major pentatonic phrase in G♭ (played a half step below the tonic center of G), John is probably thinking D7 over the whole phrase. In that case, we have the ♭9 (E♭), the 3 (G♭ or F♯), the ♭5 (A♭), and the ♯5 (B♭ or A♯). The phrase lies quite easily under the fingers on guitar and is therefore rather simple to play. This type of "outside" playing is certainly more indicative of modern players, as opposed to the classic bebop guitarists.

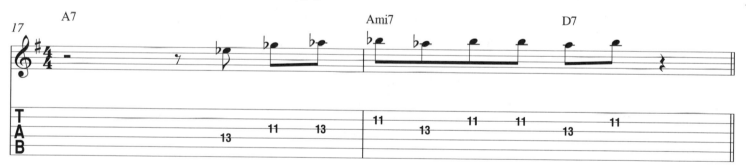

FIG. 3.1. "If I Were a Bell" Measures 17–18

The figure in measures 53–54 is interesting to analyze harmonically. It is basically a C minor pentatonic phrase with the inclusion of the major 3 of C (E). John plays this, interestingly enough, over an E7 altered chord, and again, it lays very easily under the fingers on the guitar. Starting from the E7 altered chord in measure 54, we end up with the alterations of the ♯5 (C/B♯), ♭5 (B♭), ♯9 (F double sharp/G), and the ♭9 (F natural), which makes for a very harmonically interesting phrase.

The concept of taking basic information you already know, in this case a C minor pentatonic scale, and superimposing it over different chords, is a technique that is done by all of the jazz greats, especially the modern players. This is a good example of that.

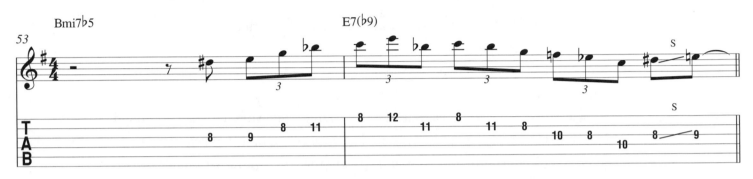

FIG. 3.2. "If I Were a Bell" Measures 53–54

The figure in measures 64–65 clearly shows John thinking F melodic minor over the E7 chord. Playing F melodic minor over an E7 chord is the same as playing the E altered scale, which is the seventh mode of F melodic minor. The "jazz" melodic minor scale is considered a more modern harmonic approach.

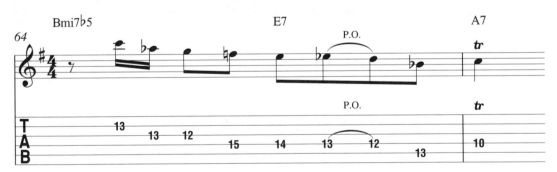

FIG. 3.3. "If I Were a Bell" Measures 64–65

If I Were a Bell
Solo by John Scofield

By Frank Loesser

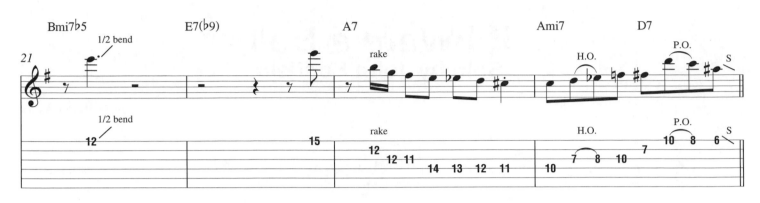

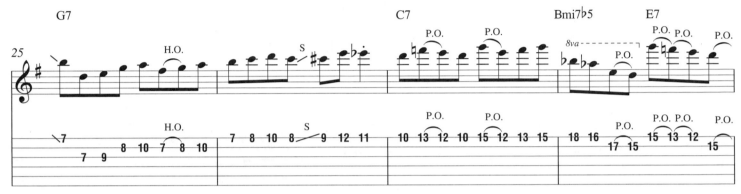

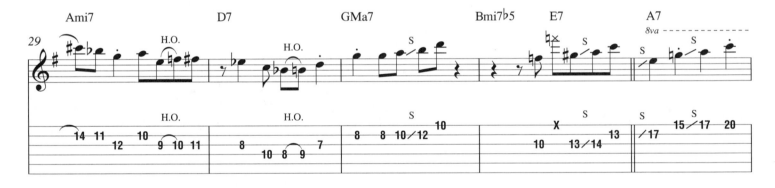

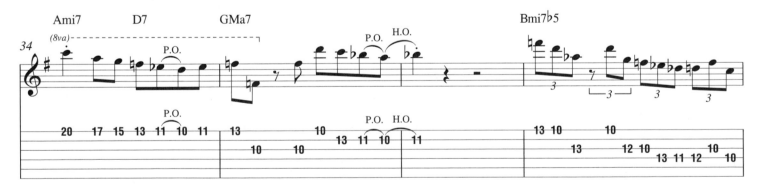

FIG. 3.4. "If I Were a Bell"

"All the Things You Are"

"All the Things You Are" was recorded on John Scofield's 1989 album *Flat Out*. The personnel included Anthony Cox on bass and Terri Lyne Carrington on drums. It is not necessarily the phrases that make John's playing modern, but the way he articulates them. John's articulation is a very modern, personal thing, and it is very difficult to replicate.

Measures 38–40 are a good example of how John negotiates his way through the turnaround and back to the top of the tune. Notice the major 3 of C (E) to the ♯9 (E♭/D♯) in measure 39 before the resolution on the 3 (A♭) of the F minor 7 chord.

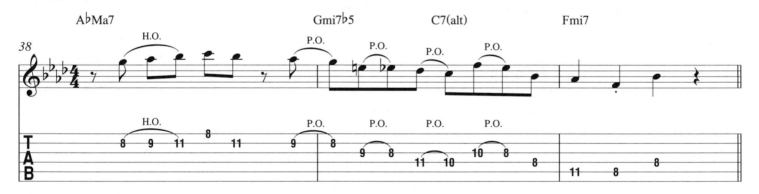

FIG. 4.1. "All the Things You Are" Measures 38–40

Measure 82 is a beautiful, simple major phrase over C major 7 with some string skipping involved.

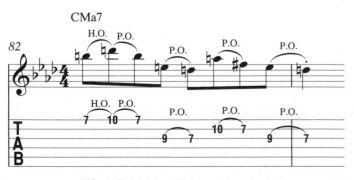

FIG. 4.2. "All the Things You Are" Measure 82

Measures 127–131 are a II V I phrase in the key of G major. Over the A minor 7 chord, we see an interval of a fifth between the first two notes of G and D in measure 128, which then goes to the 3 (B). Next, John goes down a half step to an F♯ while keeping the rest of the idea the same. In the next measure (129), over the D7 chord, we see an interesting chromatic idea from E to E♭, back to E, then F and F♯, before the phrase continues up the first three notes of the D Mixolydian scale. The resolution to the G major 7 chord is delayed until the second measure of the chord. This phrase contains many elements of both classic and modern jazz such as a motif in measure 128, chromaticism in measure 129, and a delayed resolution on the I chord. Again, it is John's articulation that is so modern and incredible.

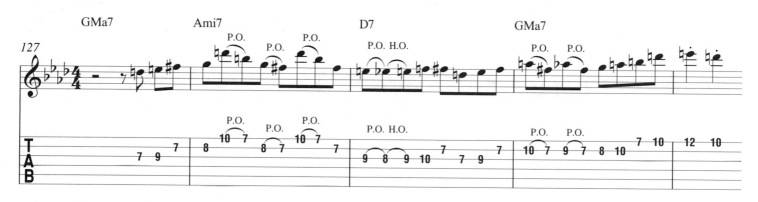

FIG. 4.3. "All the Things You Are" Measures 127–131

Measures 200–203 are another II V I phrase, also in G. Look at the alterations of the D7 chord. There is a ♯5 (A♯), a ♭9 (F/E♯), and a ♭5 (A♭). Over the G major 7 chord, he starts with an A minor triad followed by a diminished 7 arpeggio starting on B♭. Again, as with the previous example, the resolution to the I chord doesn't happen until the second measure.

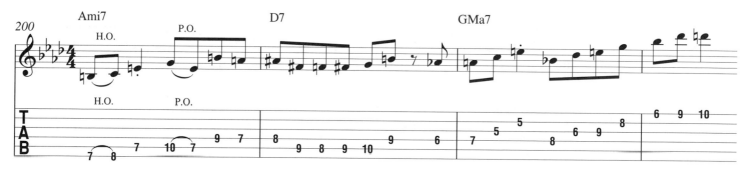

FIG. 4.4. "All the Things You Are" Measures 200–203

All the Things You Are
Solo by John Scofield

Lyrics by Oscar Hammerstein II
Music by Jerome Kern

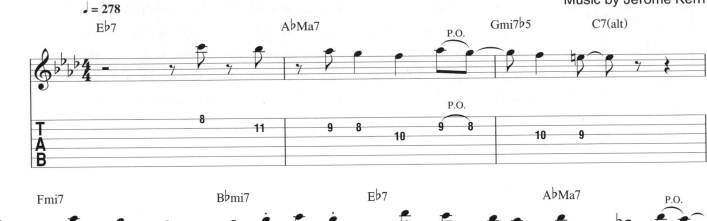

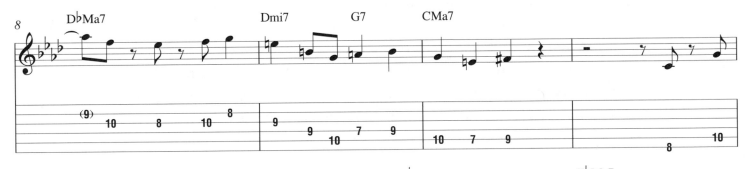

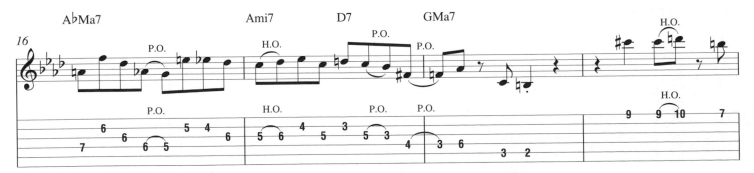

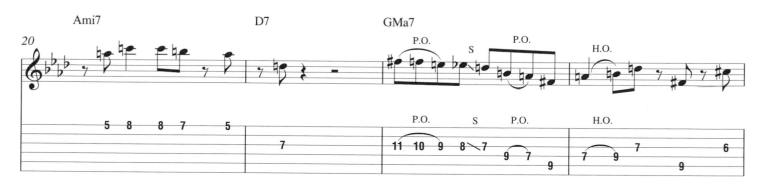

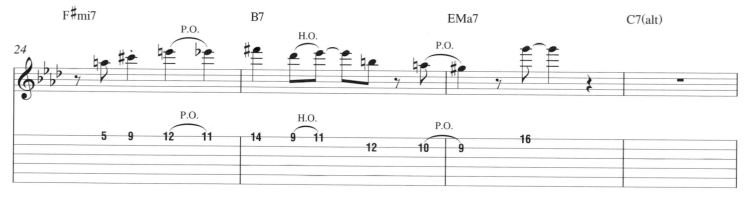

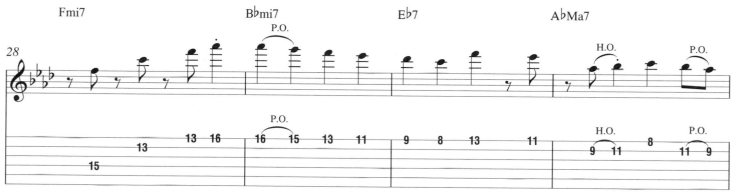

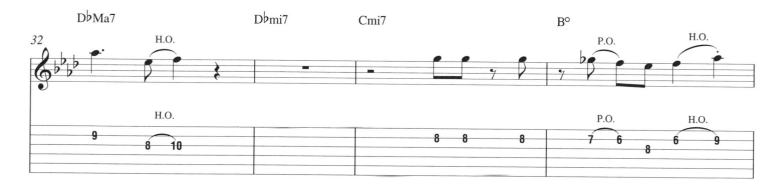

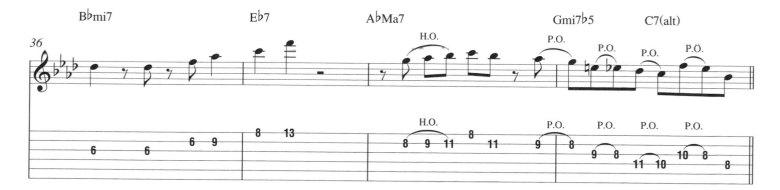

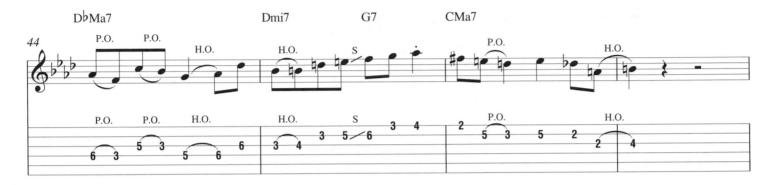

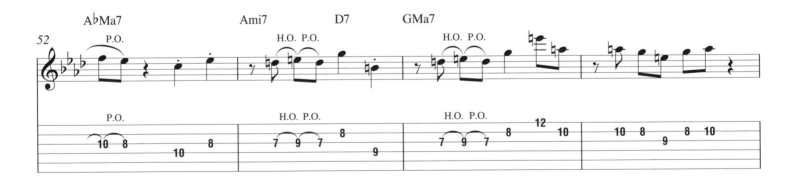

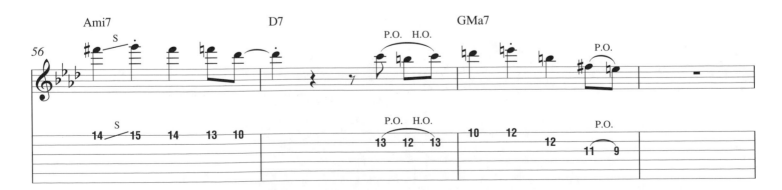

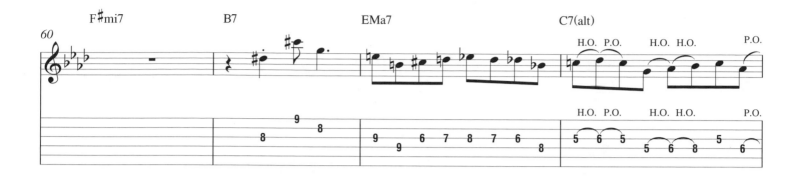

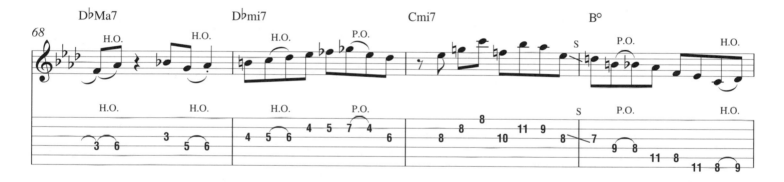

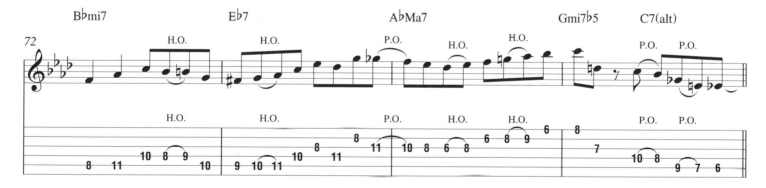

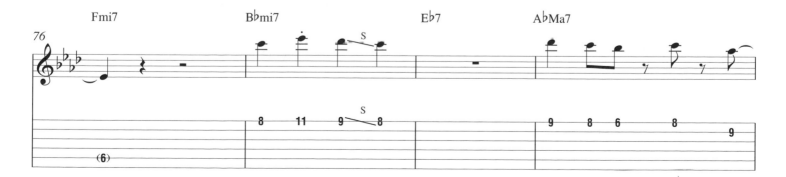

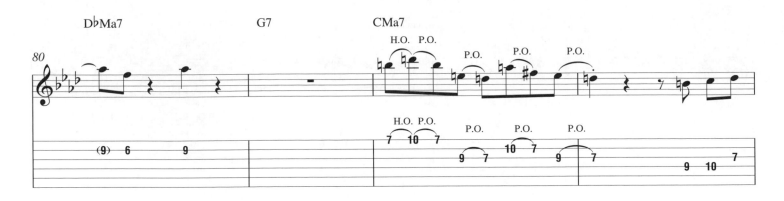

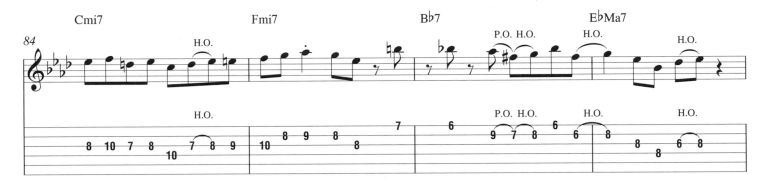

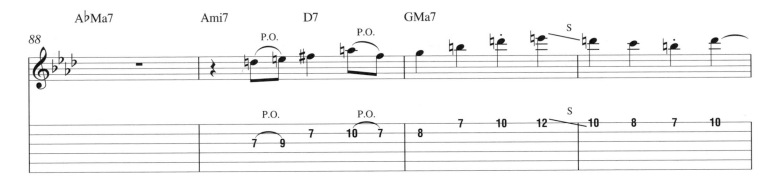

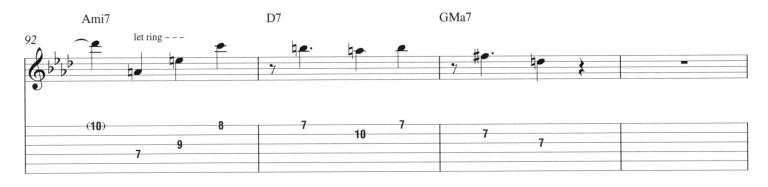

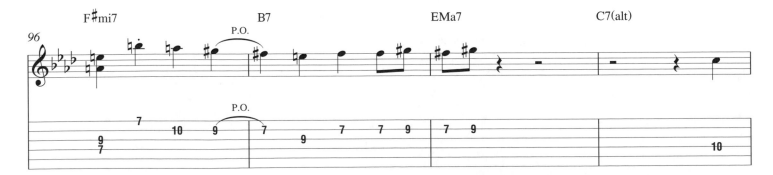

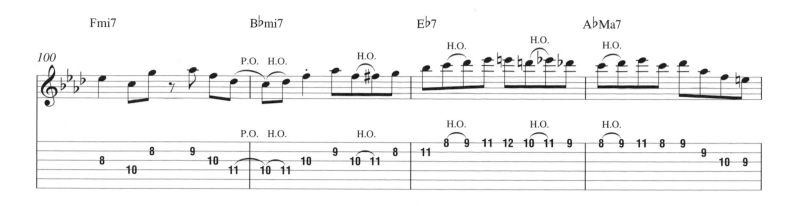

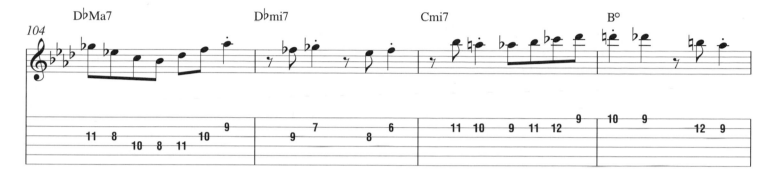

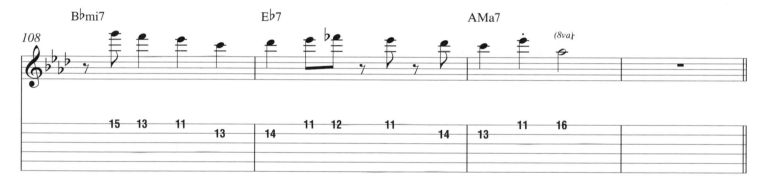

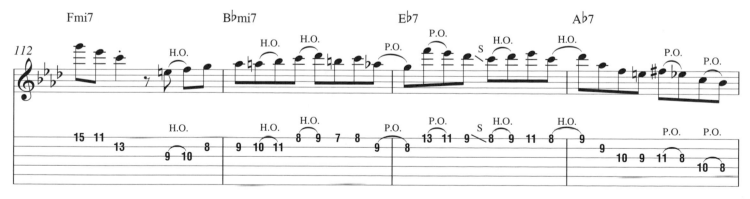

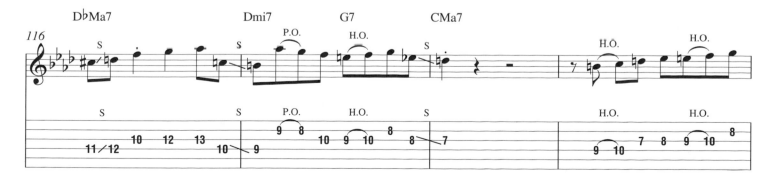

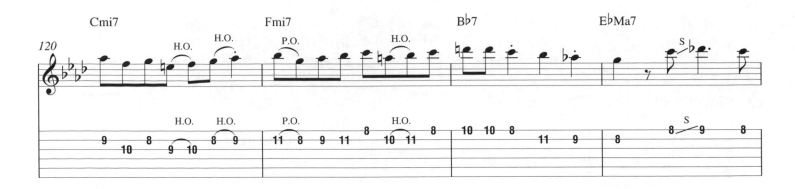

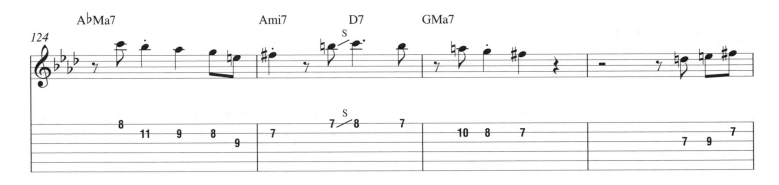

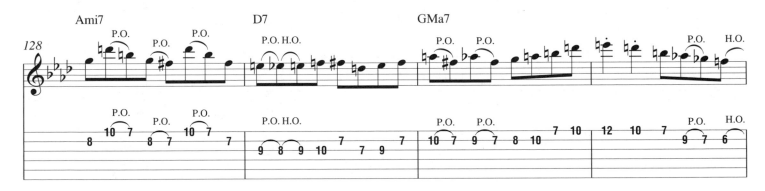

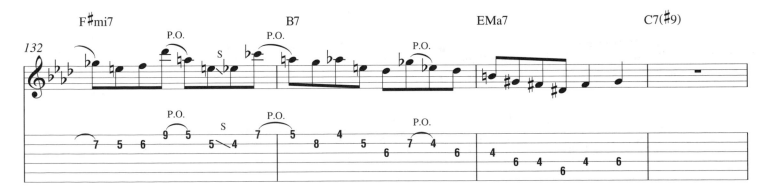

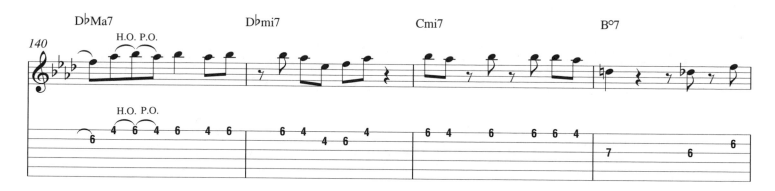

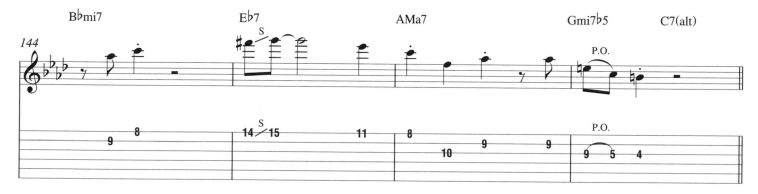

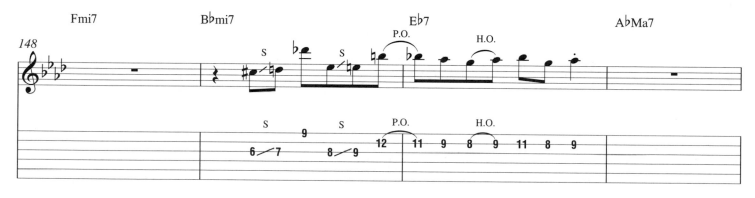

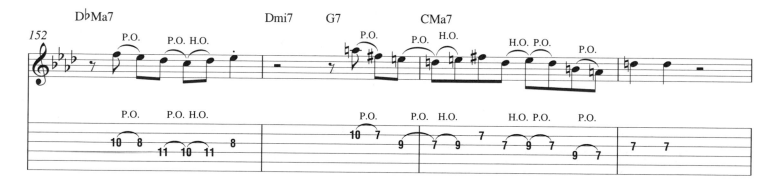

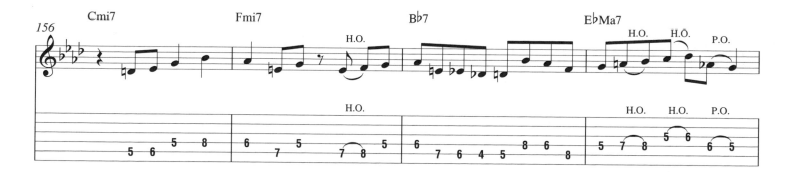

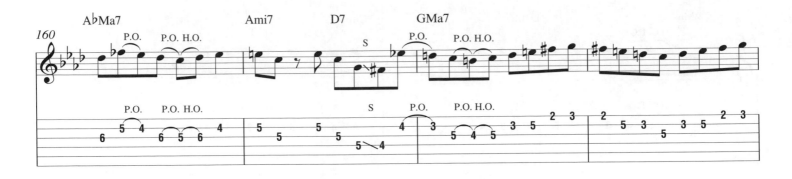

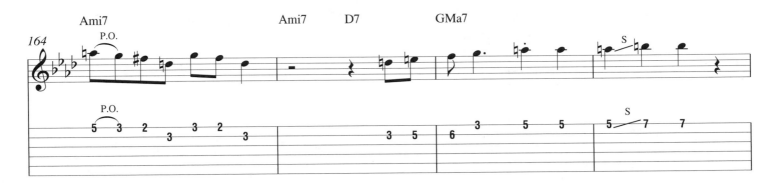

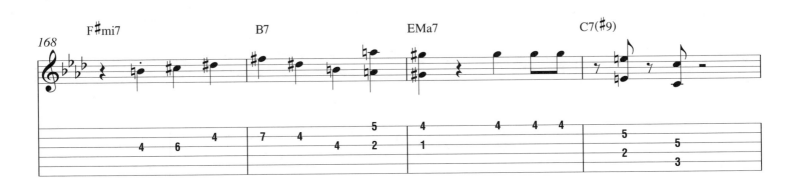

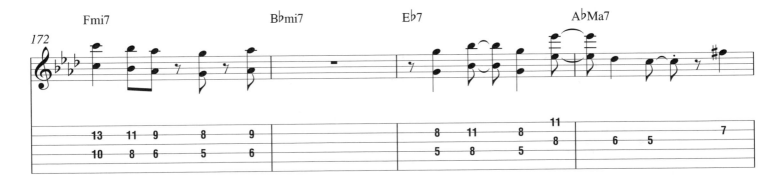

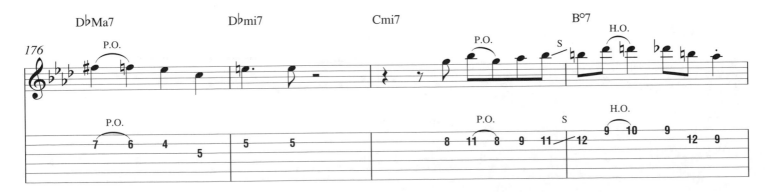

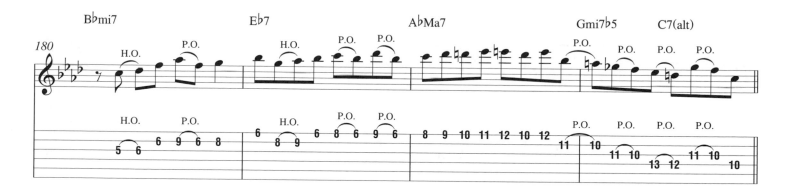

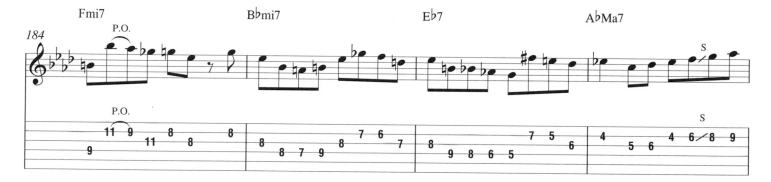

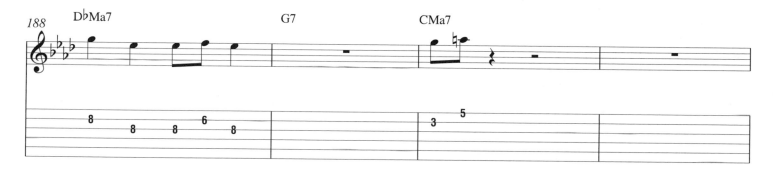

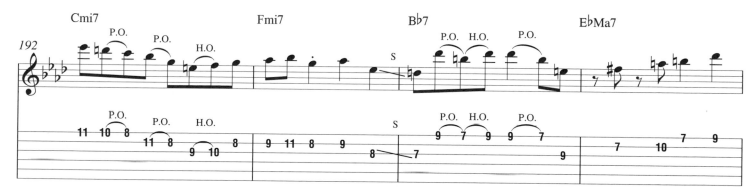

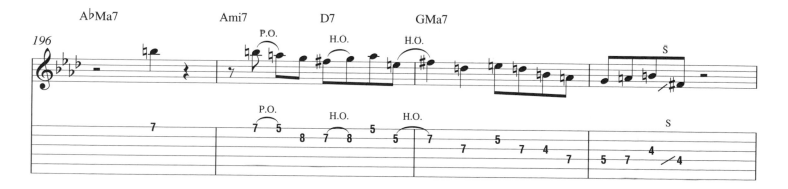

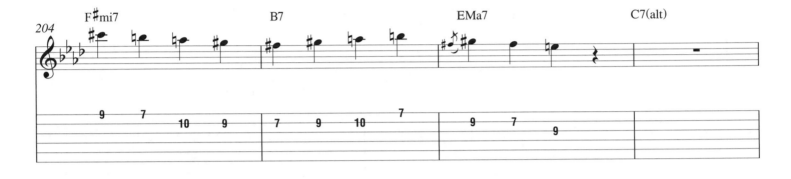

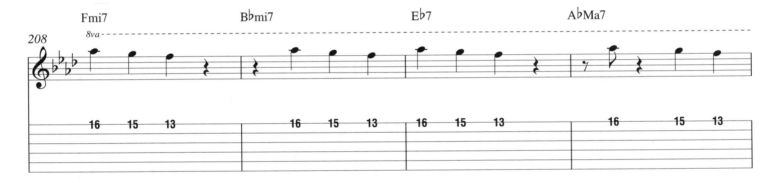

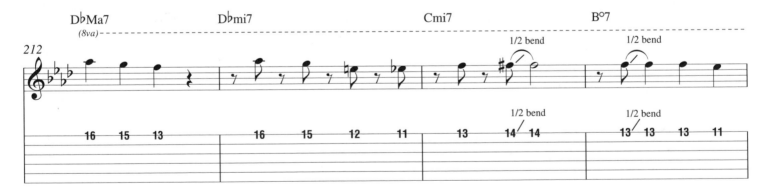

FIG. 4.5. "All the Things You Are"

5. PAT MARTINO

"Impressions"

"Impressions" was recorded on Pat Martino's album *Consciousness*. It was released in 1974 and features Eddie Green on electric piano, Tyrone Brown on bass, and Sherman Ferguson on drums. Pat plays the tune in A minor as opposed to the original key of D minor. As indicative of Pat's playing style in this solo, we are bombarded with a barrage of eighth notes, mostly articulated with the pick yet still swinging hard. This kind of articulation is unheard of in the classic bebop jazz guitar players.

Measures 35–36 illustrate Pat using a very common phrase that is quite easy to play on the instrument. It shows him using a descending C minor 7 arpeggio starting from the 7 (B♭) followed by a descending G minor 7 arpeggio starting from the 7 (F).

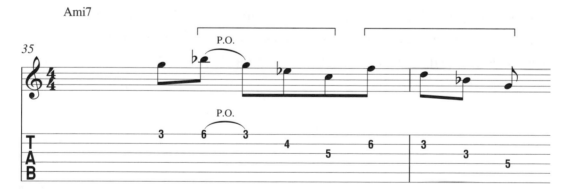

FIG. 5.1. "Impressions" Measures 35–36

Measures 71–75 outline an A minor-major 7 chord using the 3 (C), the 5 (E), the ♯7 (G♯), and the 9 (B). He starts from the 3 and goes down the arpeggio starting with the B, and playing the same phrase six times. Notice how it is also a C+Maj7 (C, E, G♯, B) arpeggio in root position.

FIG. 5.2. "Impressions" Measures 71–75

Measures 82–89 use a simple B♭ minor 9 (B♭, D♭, F, and A♭) arpeggio with the inclusion of the 11 (E♭) a few times. This phrase was selected because of the interesting rhythm that Pat used. Sometimes, the simplest ideas can be very hip and modern sounding if played with an interesting rhythm.

FIG. 5.3. "Impressions" Measures 82–89

Impressions
Solo by Pat Martino

By John Coltrane

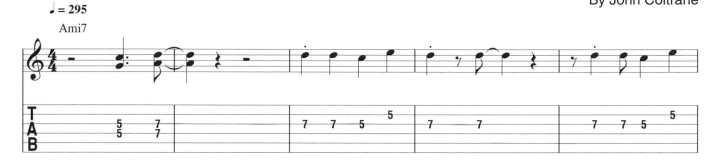

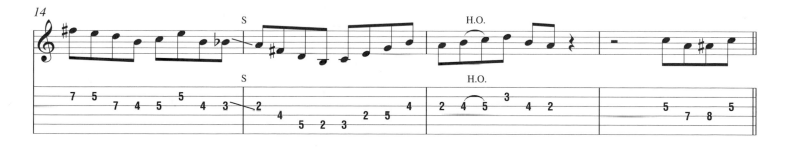

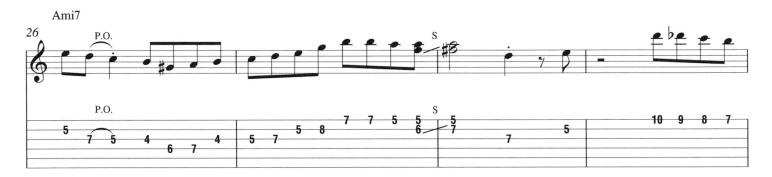

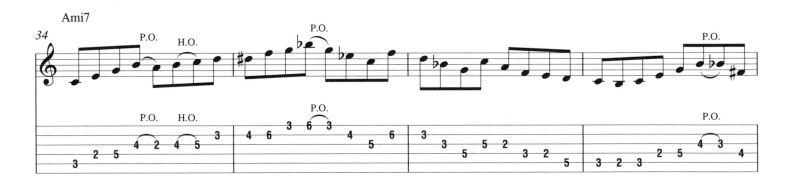

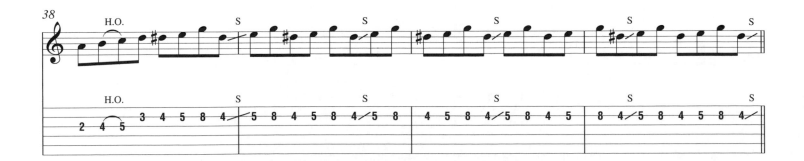

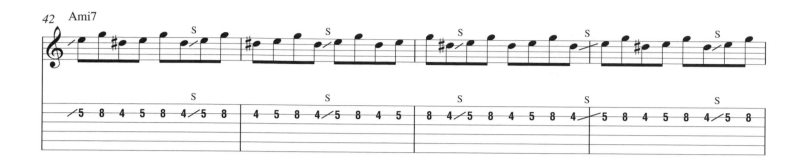

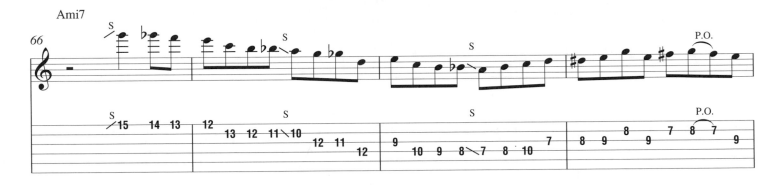

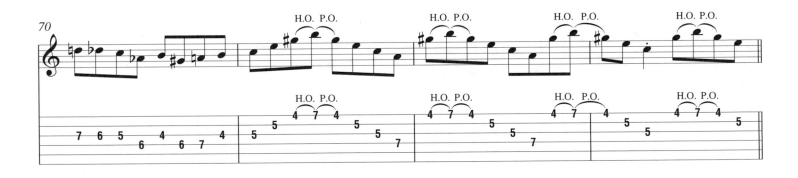

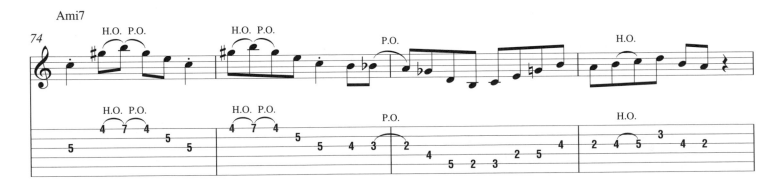

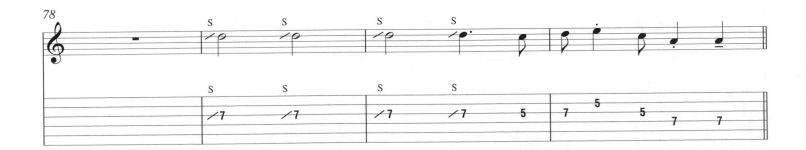

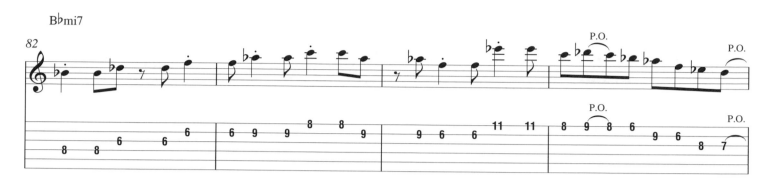

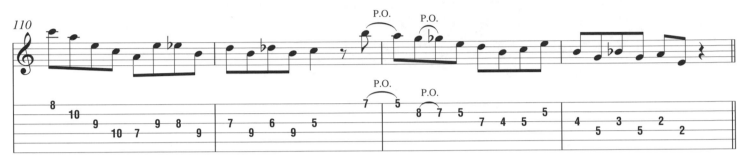

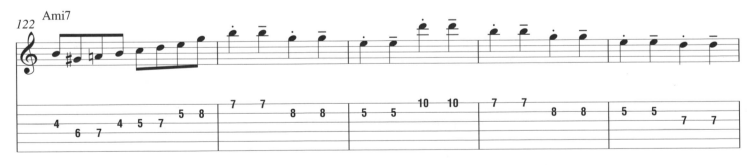

FIG. 5.4. "Impressions"

6. PAT MARTINO

"Oleo"

"Oleo" is from Pat Martino's GRAMMY® nominated album *Live at Yoshi's*. It was recorded live on December 15 to 17, 2000 at Yoshi's Jazz House in Oakland, California. It features Pat in an organ trio setting with Joey DeFrancesco on the B3 Hammond organ and Billy Hart on drums. Pat abandons the traditional "Rhythm Changes" for the A section, and chooses to solo over C minor.

Measures 43–47 is a great example of what is called "side stepping." Side stepping is a modern concept where you "side step" out by a half step before returning to the original key. For example, playing in a scale a half-step above or below a given chord, before resolving, creating tension and release. In this case, Pat side steps into D♭ minor before resolving back to C minor.

FIG. 6.1. "Oleo" Measures 43–47

At measure 105, Pat goes up a minor third, from C minor to E♭ minor, and plays an E♭ minor phrase to create tension before resolving to C. Although occasionally used in the bebop style, this is considered a modern (contemporary) concept of the jazz language.

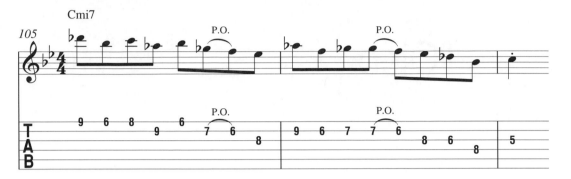

FIG. 6.2. "Oleo" Measures 105–107

The section beginning at measure 130 lasts for fifteen measures. Playing the same phrase over and over again can be challenging for many reasons. First, at a fast tempo, it is difficult to keep consistent. Second, many improvisers feel that they will bore their fellow musicians and audience by over-repeating the same phrase. However, as you can hear in the recording, Pat plays this phrase beautifully, and when it finally resolves, the listener feels a great sense of release.

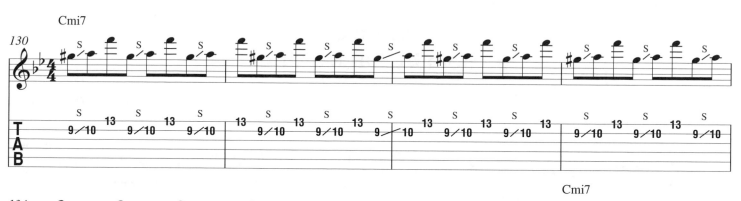

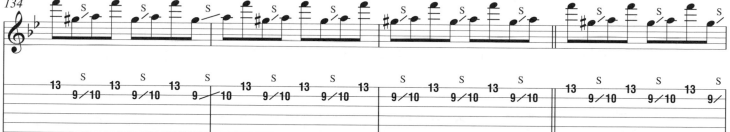

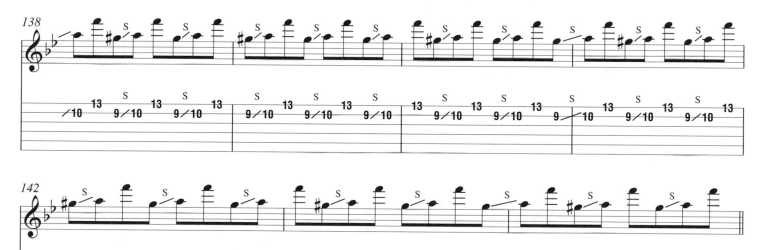

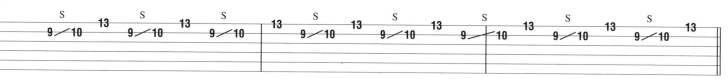

FIG. 6.3. "Oleo" Measures 130–144

Oleo
Solo by Pat Martino

By Sonny Rollins

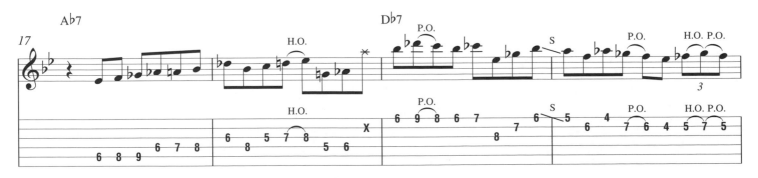

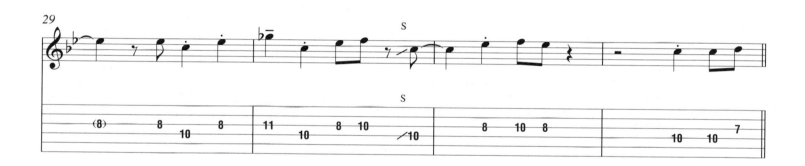

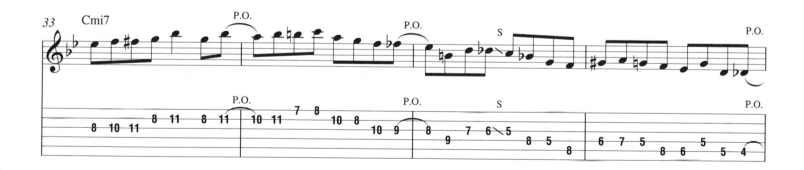

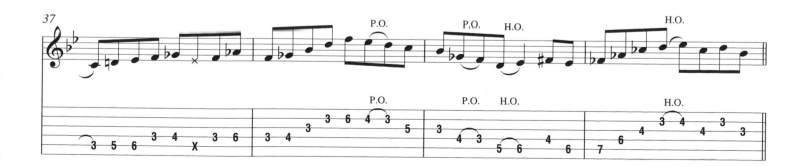

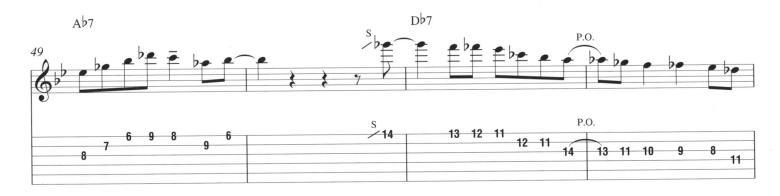

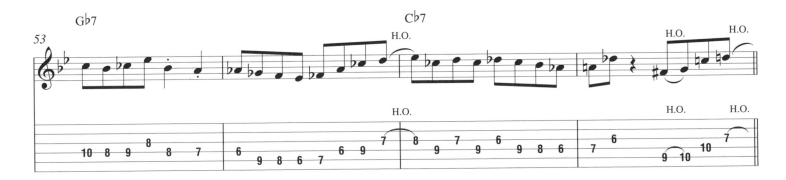

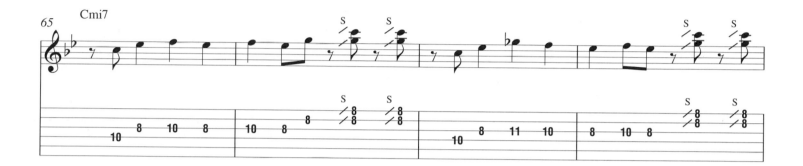

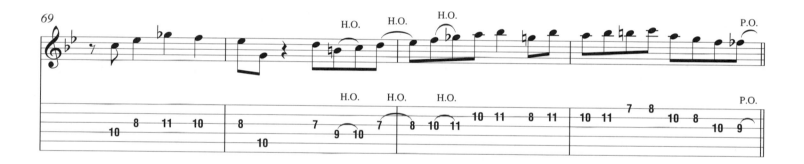

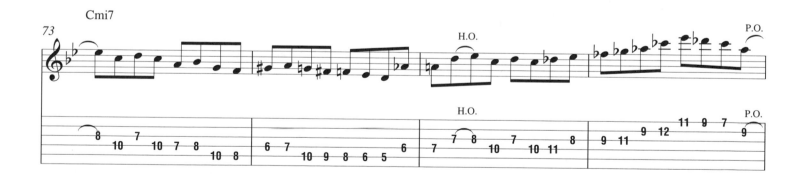

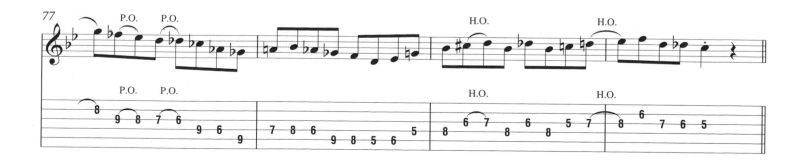

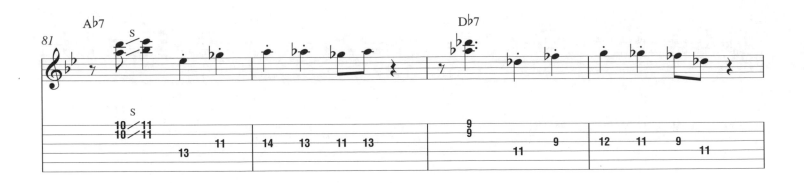

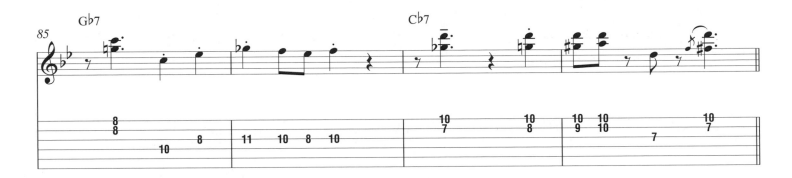

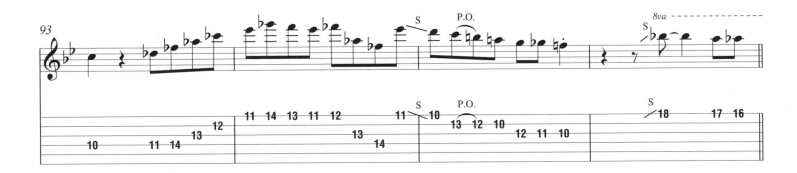

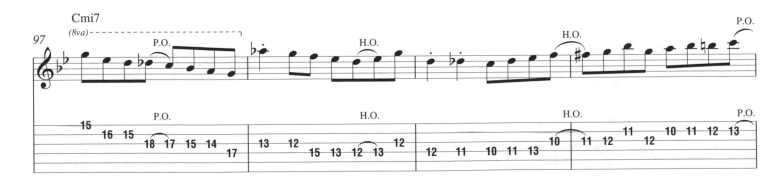

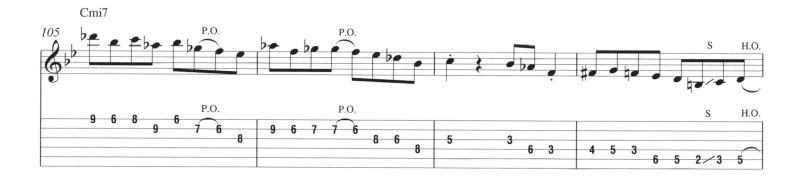

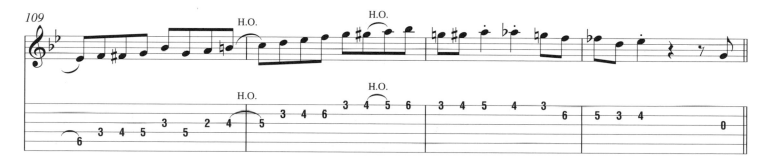

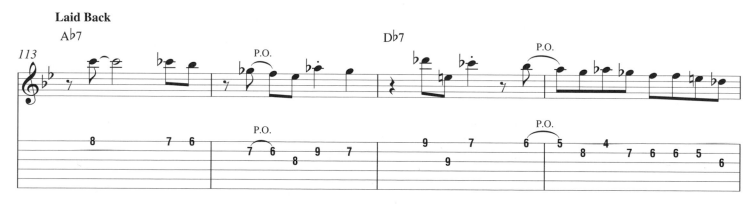

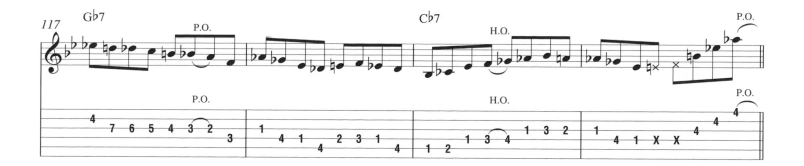

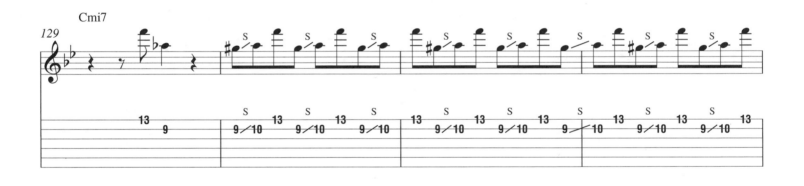

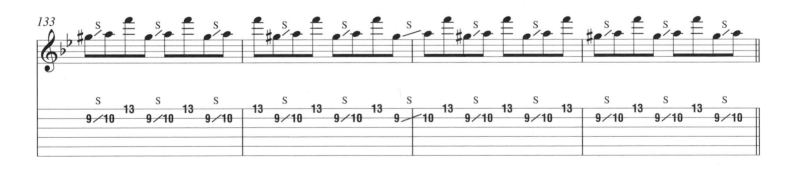

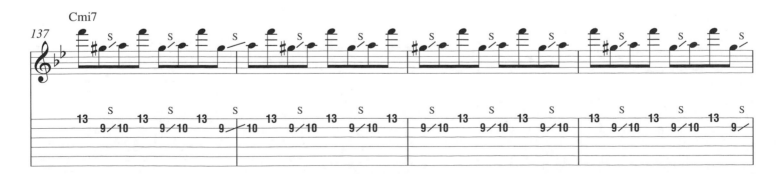

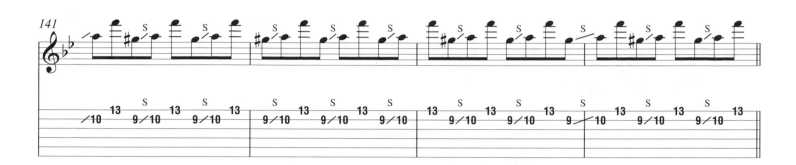

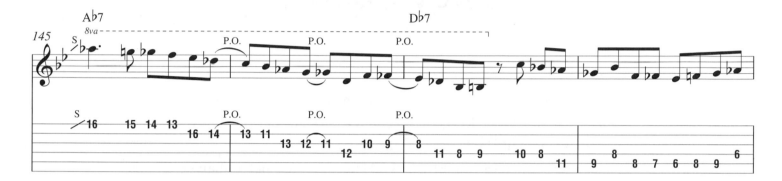

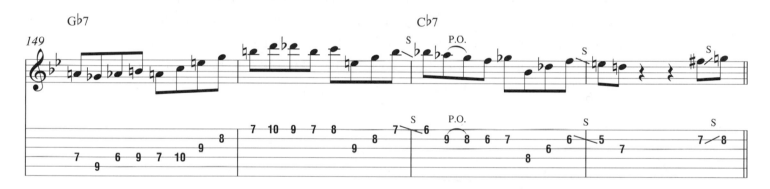

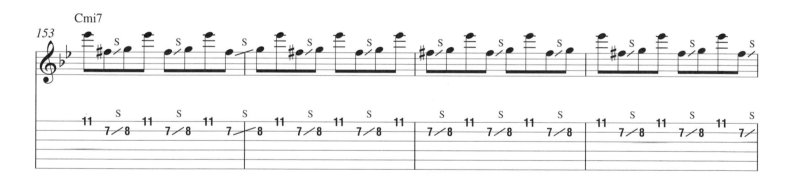

FIG. 6.4. "Oleo"

7. KURT ROSENWINKEL

"Dewey Square"

"Dewey Square" was recorded on Kurt's second album as a band leader, entitled *Intuit*. The album was released in 1999. It includes Joe Martin on bass, Michael Kanan on piano, and Tim Pleasant on drums.

The analysis of measures 21–22 reveals Kurt thinking of F Lydian dominant, which is the fourth mode of C melodic minor. Lydian dominant is a very modern sound. He uses an E♭ major 7♯5 arpeggio in root position followed by a C minor-major 7 arpeggio. You can clearly see an F7(♯11) chord idea with a few color tones. He starts from the 7 (E♭) and then plays the 9 (G), ♯11 (B), and the 13 (D) before hitting the 5 (C), which is followed by the 7, 9, ♯11, and 13 again.

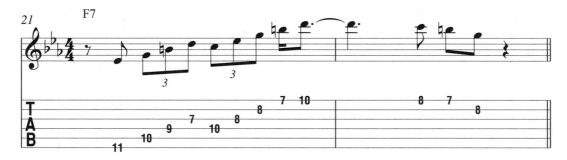

FIG. 7.1. "Dewey Square" Measures 21–22

In measures 32–33, Kurt uses the triad pairs of F major and G major over the E♭ major 7 chord. Triad pairs are a very hip, modern sound that was not used often by the more traditional bebop players.

FIG. 7.2. "Dewey Square" Measures 32–33

Measures 84–86 show many alterations on the F7 chord. He uses Lydian dominant again, the ♯11 (B natural) starting in measure 84, followed by the ♯9 (G♯/A♭), and the ♭9 (G♭/F♯).

FIG. 7.3. "Dewey Square" Measures 84–86

In measures 91–97, Kurt ends his solo with a nice run with a lot of chromaticism. Although chromaticism is used in all styles of jazz, typically, the more modern the style, the more chromaticism can be found.

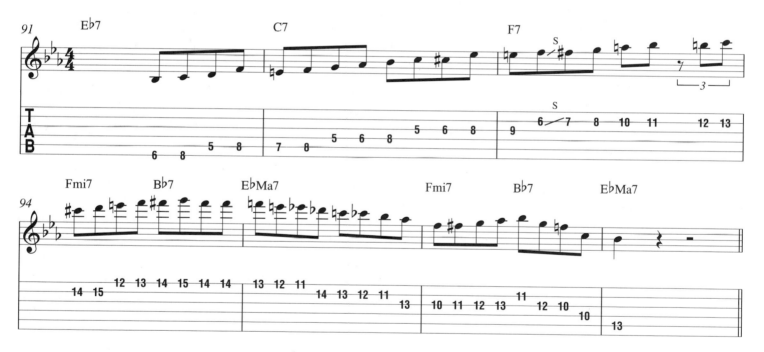

FIG. 7.4. "Dewey Square" Measures 91–97

Dewey Square
Solo by Kurt Rosenwinkel

By Charlie Parker

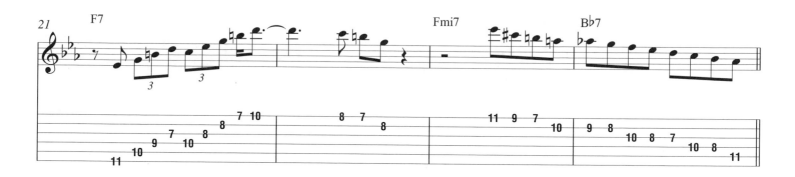

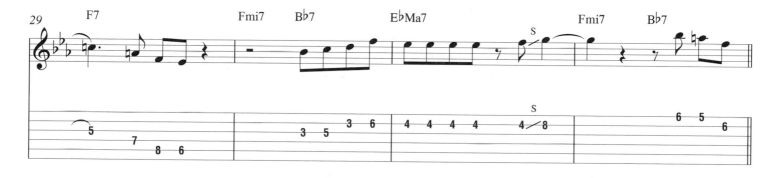

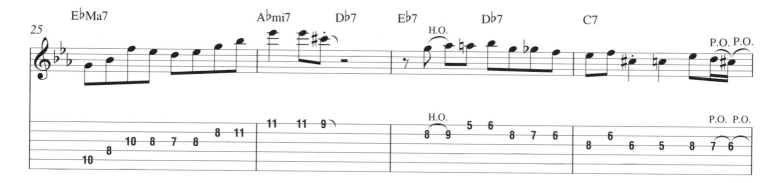

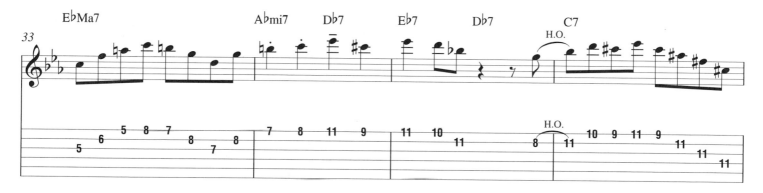

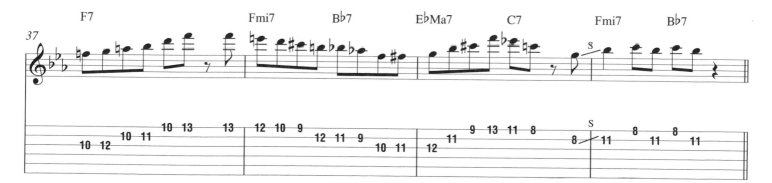

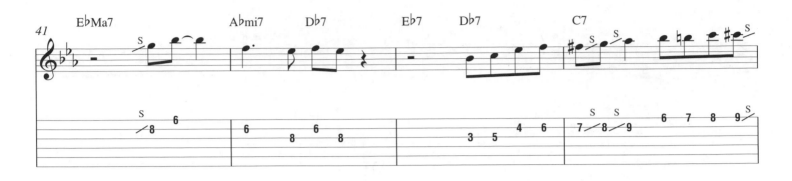

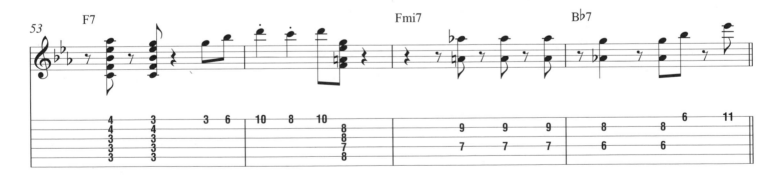

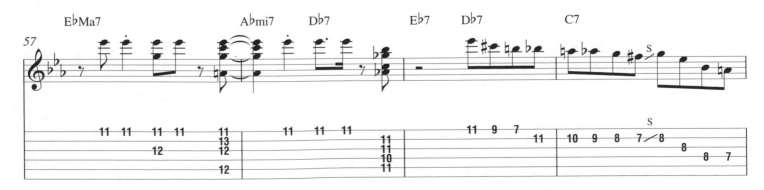

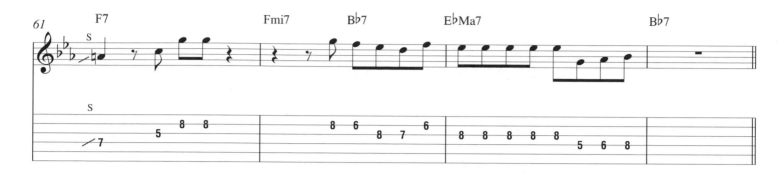

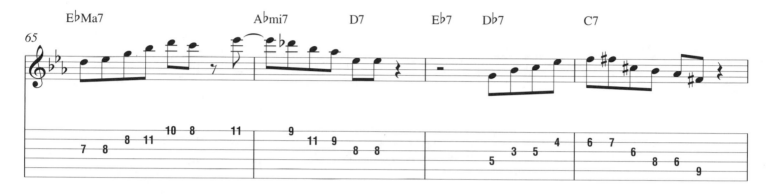

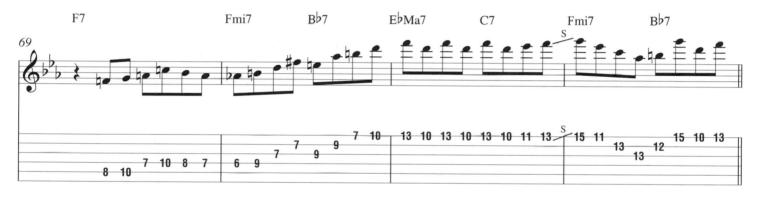

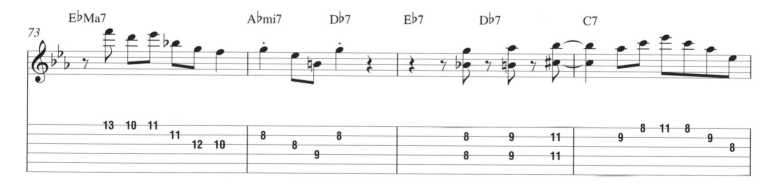

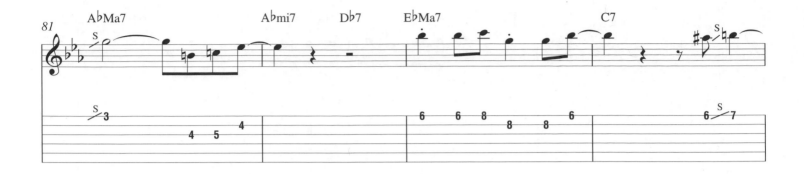

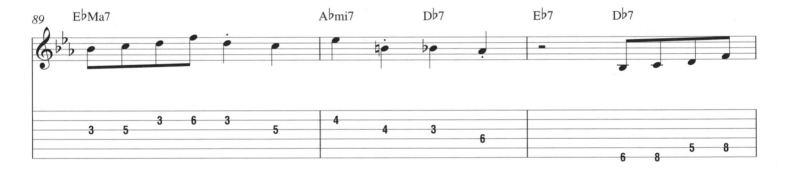

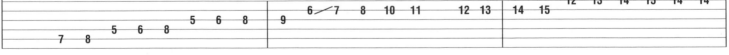

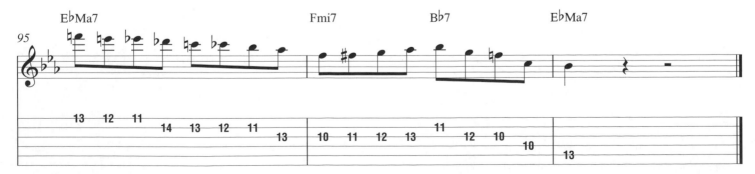

FIG. 7.5. "Dewey Square"

8. KURT ROSENWINKEL

"How Deep Is the Ocean"

"How Deep Is the Ocean" also comes from Kurt's *Intuit* album. Kurt is a master of using basic triads in his solo improvisations. We explore how he uses them in this solo.

Measures 1–3 show Kurt using four triads. First a descending A♭ major triad followed by an ascending B♭ major triad. Next, he uses a descending D♭ major triad followed by an ascending E♭ major triad. Again, using triad pairs is a very modern sound.

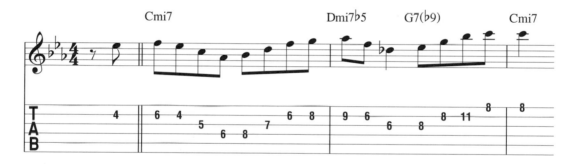

FIG. 8.1. "How Deep Is the Ocean" Measures 1–3

Measures 6–9 uses again the A♭ major and B♭ major triads for the first two measures, followed by an F♯ major triad and an E major triad.

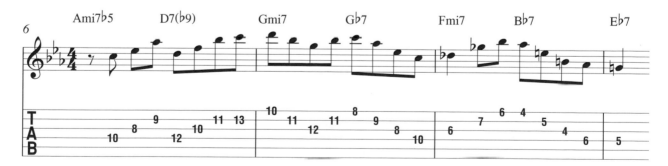

FIG. 8.2. "How Deep Is the Ocean" Measures 6–9

Measures 80–82 use six different triads: a G major triad, an A diminished triad, a B diminished triad, a C minor triad, a D minor triad, and an E♭ major triad.

FIG. 8.3. "How Deep Is the Ocean" Measures 80–82

How Deep Is the Ocean
(How High Is the Sky)
Solo by Kurt Rosenwinkel

Words and Music by
Irving Berlin

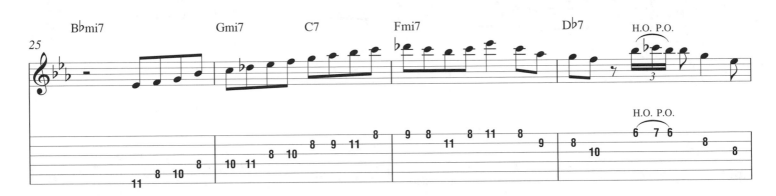

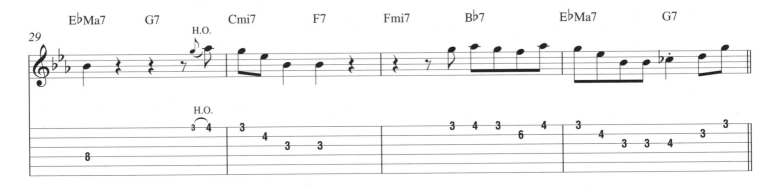

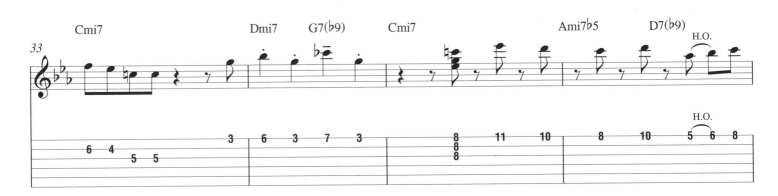

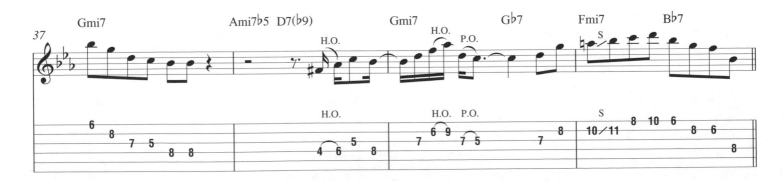

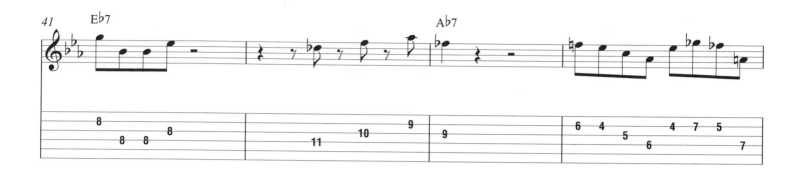

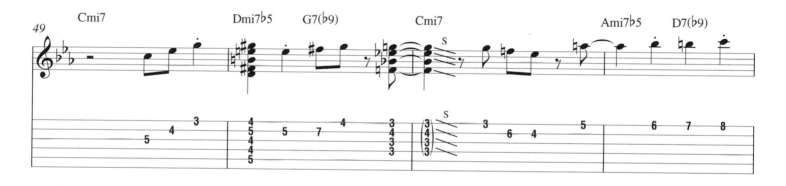

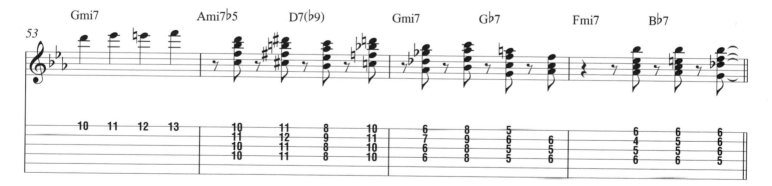

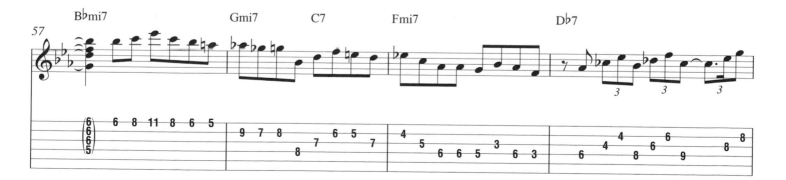

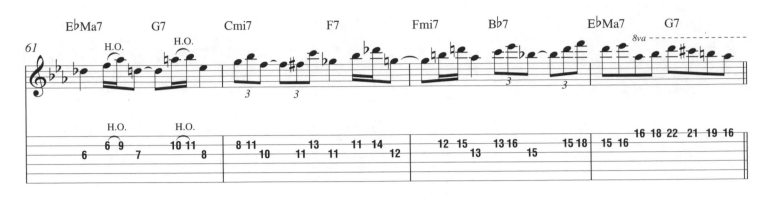

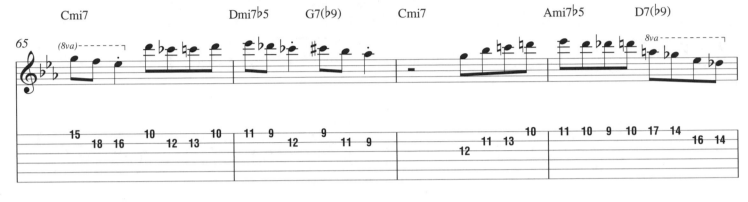

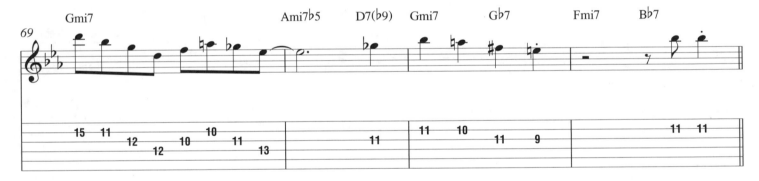

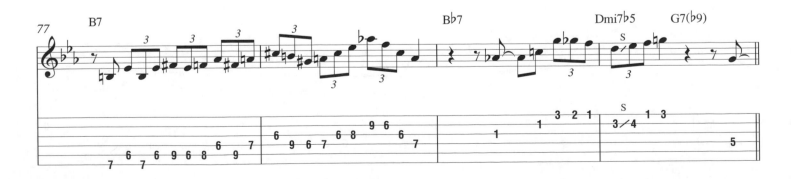

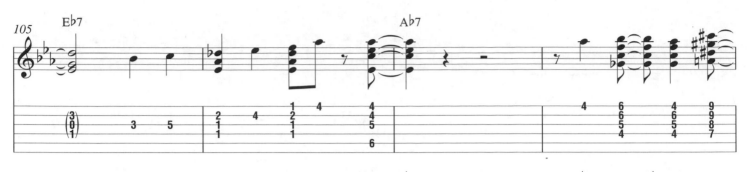

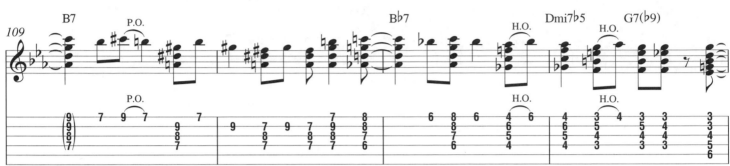

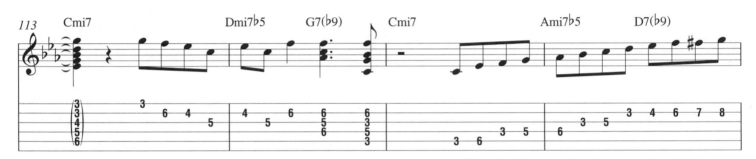

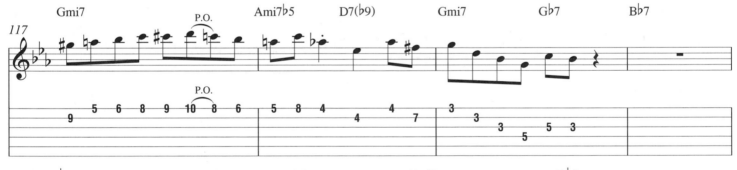

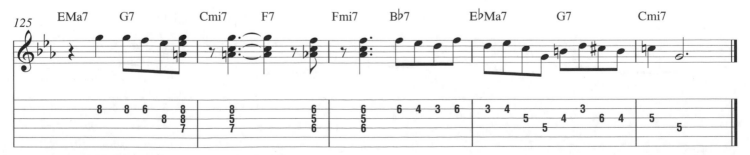

FIG. 8.4. "How Deep Is the Ocean"

9. BIRÉLI LAGRÈNE

"Donna Lee"

"Donna Lee" comes from Biréli Lagrène's *Standards* album. It was recorded and released in 1992 and features bassist Niels Pedersen and drummer André Ceccarelli. In this solo, we will look at a II V I phrase in the key of A♭. All of the licks are relatively the same, with the exception of the resolution on the A♭ major 7 chord.

Measures 63–65 start with a 1, 2, 3, 5 Coltrane idea in A♭. (There is no doubt that John Coltrane is considered to be a pioneer of modern jazz.) Then, Biréli plays a 3, 5, 7, and ♭9 of F7. Starting with the measure of E♭7, we see a 3, 5, 7, and ♭9 of B♭7 followed by the same of E♭7. The resolution on A♭ is an A♭ major pentatonic lick.

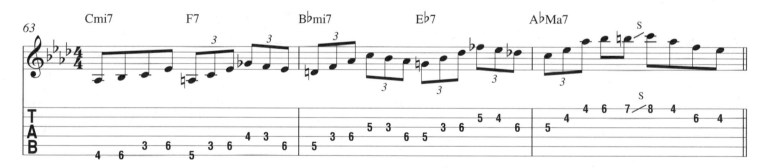

FIG. 9.1. "Donna Lee" Measures 63–65

Measures 95–97 (figure 9.2) are very similar to measures 63–65 (figure 9.1), with the exception of the first four notes of measure 95, where we see an A♭ major triad instead of the 1, 2, 3, 5 Coltrane idea from measure 63. Measure 96 is identical to measure 64. In measure 97, which is the resolution to the I chord (A♭Ma7), Biréli plays an A♭ major triad again starting from the 3 (C) followed by alternating between the minor 3 of A♭ (C♭/B natural) and the major 3 again (C).

FIG. 9.2. "Donna Lee" Measures 95–97

Measures 127–129 is the same as the previous two, only an octave higher and resolving on the A♭ major 7 chord with an A♭ blues scale.

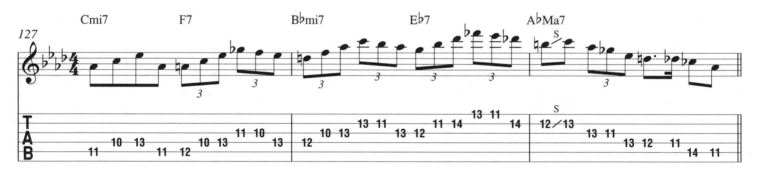

FIG. 9.3. "Donna Lee" Measures 127–129

Donna Lee
Solo by Biréli Lagrène

By Charlie Parker

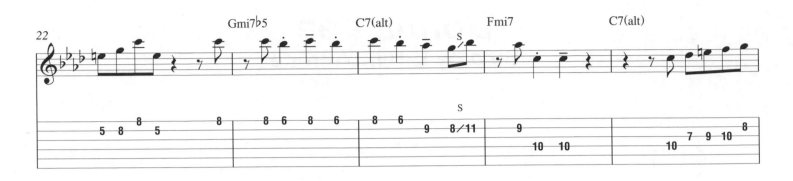

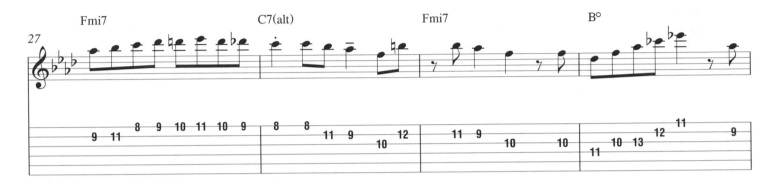

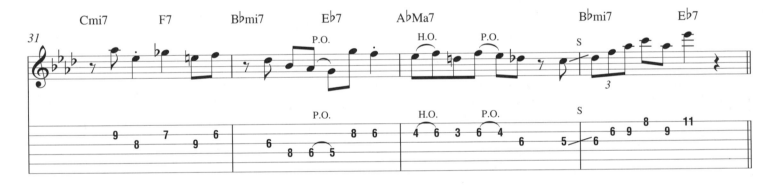

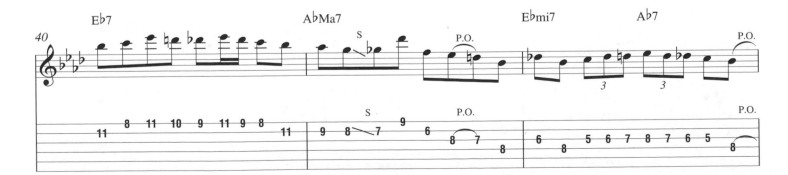

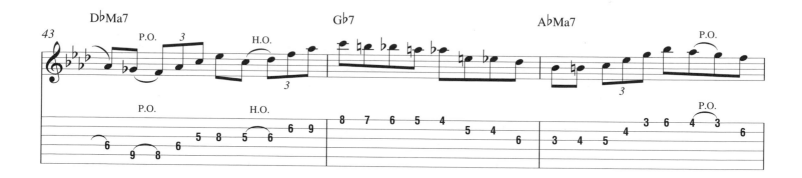

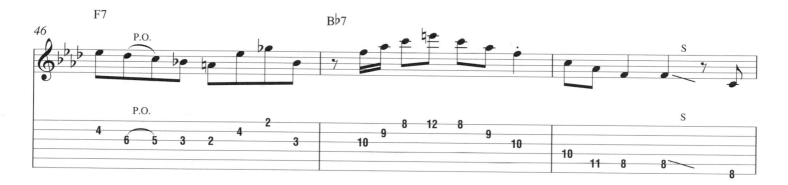

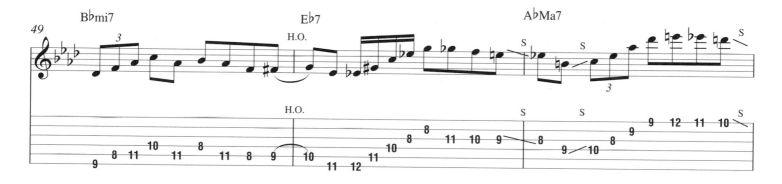

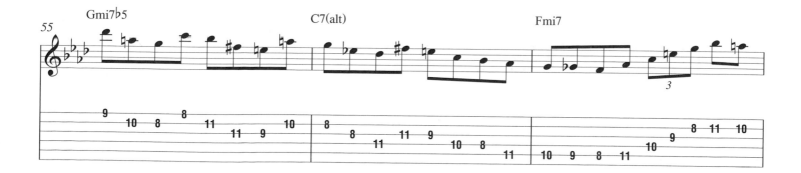

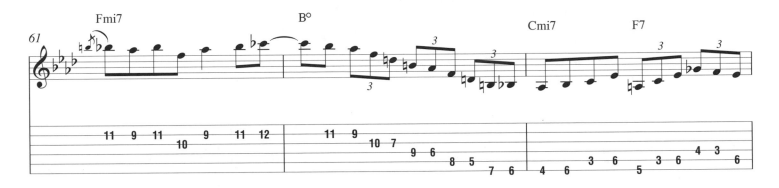

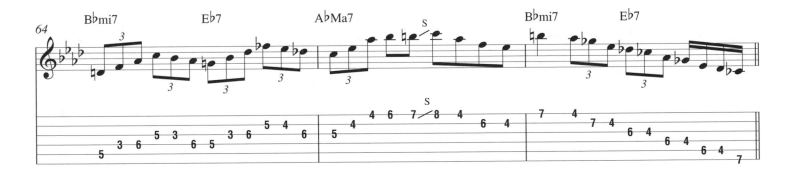

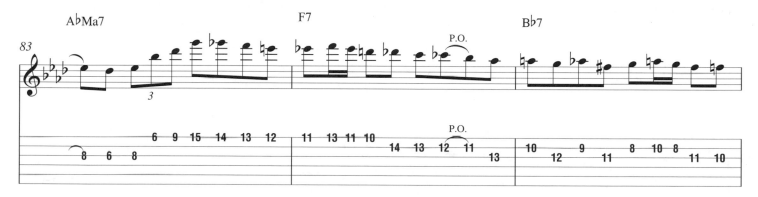

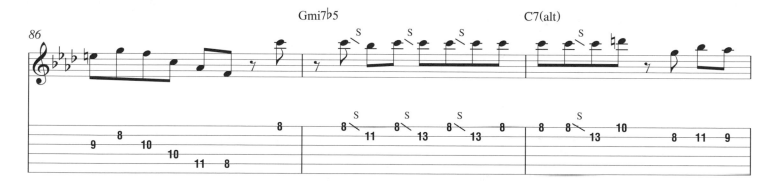

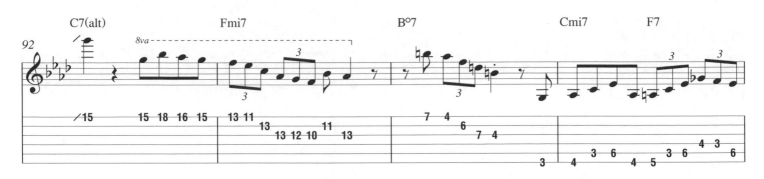

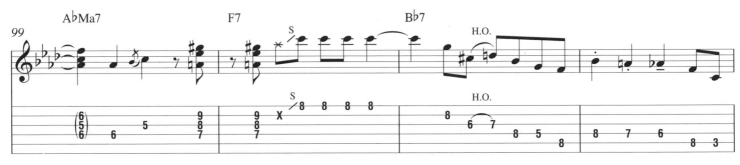

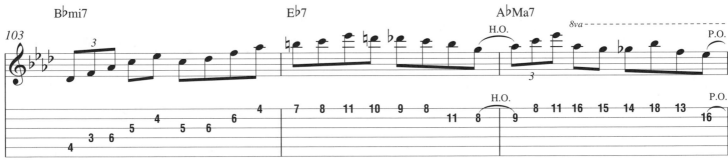

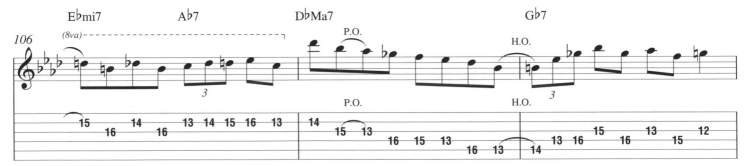

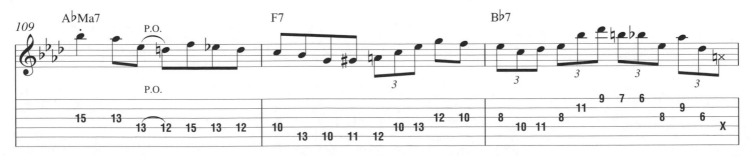

FIG. 9.4. "Donna Lee"

10. BIRÉLI LAGRÈNE

"Days of Wine and Roses"

"Days of Wine and Roses" is also on Biréli's *Standards* album. Measures 14–15 show Biréli playing a II V phrase with incredibly interesting rhythm.

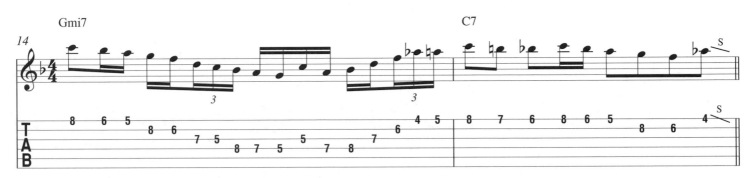

FIG. 10.1. "Days of Wine and Roses" Measures 14–15

The F blues scale is used in measures 32–34. Biréli also adds in the major 6 (D), which gives the end of the phrase an F major pentatonic feel.

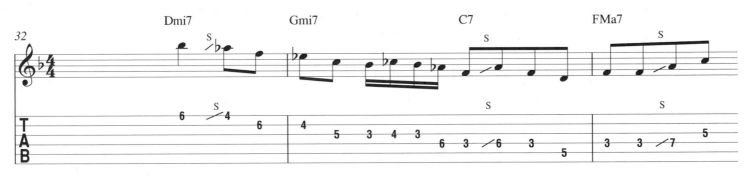

FIG. 10.2. "Days of Wine and Roses" Measures 32–34

Measures 39–40 include a diminished seventh chord functioning as a D7(♭9) chord going up in minor thirds (three frets) until the resolution on G minor 7. This concept has been used by many great jazz guitarists, including Wes Montgomery.

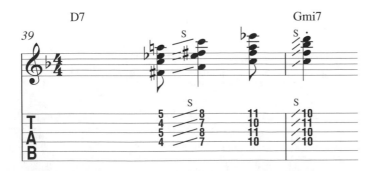

FIG. 10.3. "Days of Wine and Roses" Measures 39–40

Days of Wine and Roses
Solo by Biréli Lagrène

Lyrics by Johnny Mercer
Music by Henry Mancini

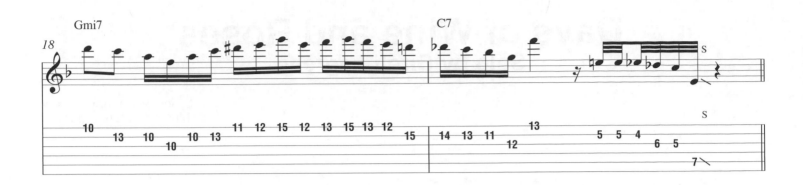

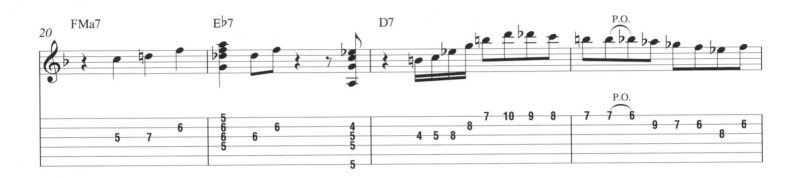

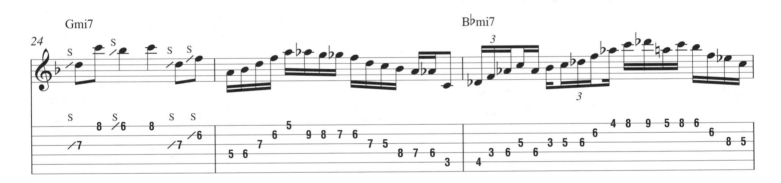

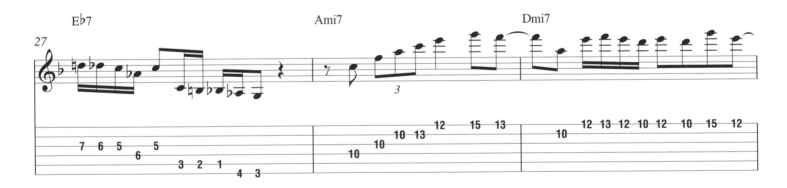

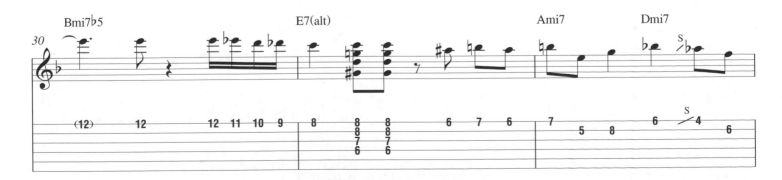

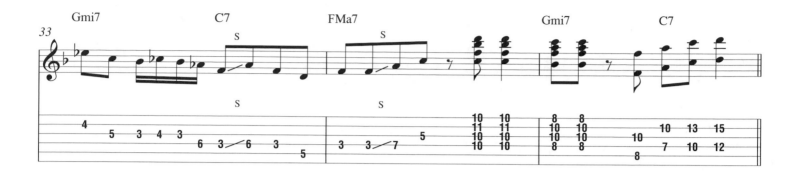

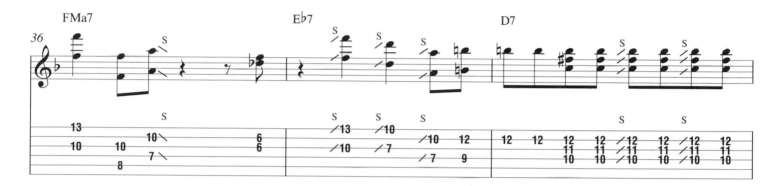

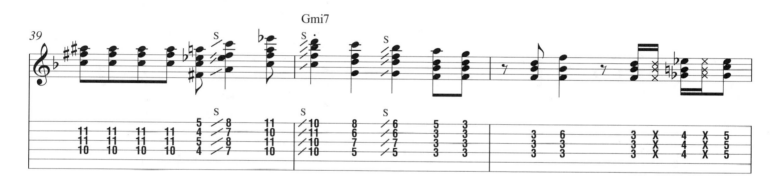

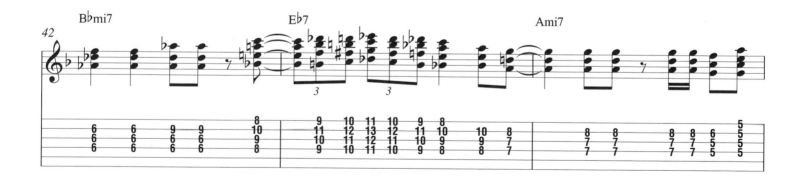

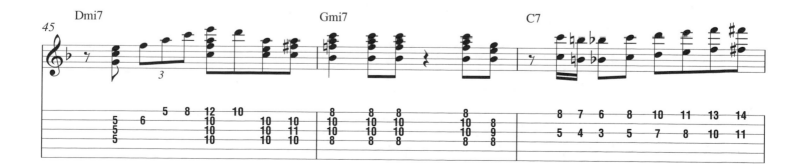

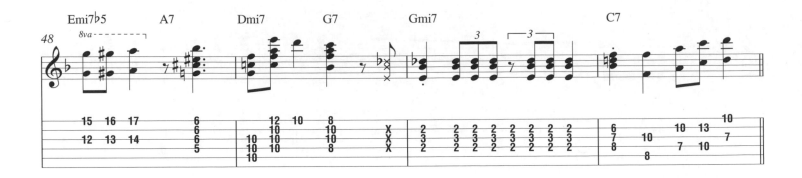

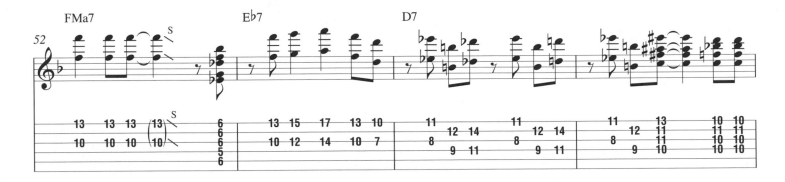

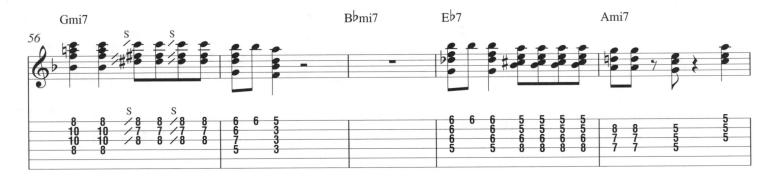

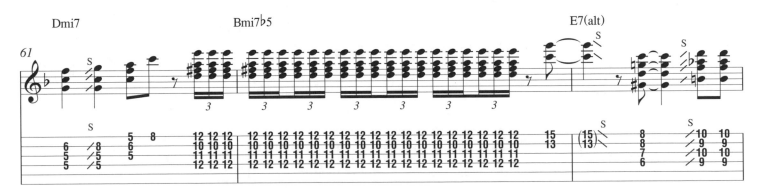

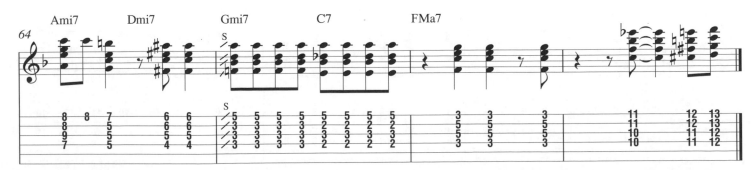

FIG. 10.4. "Days of Wine and Roses"

11. MIKE STERN

"Moment's Notice"

"Moment's Notice" is on Mike Stern's *Standards (and Other Songs)* album from 1992. It was Mike's sixth release as a leader, and this track has Al Foster on drums and Jay Anderson on bass. We will look at a Coltranesque idea, as well as one example using arpeggios.

Measures 59–63 is the classic 1, 2, 3, 5 Coltrane idea with a twist. It is over a II V chord progression in the key of C major. Mike starts on the 5 of C (G), then plays the 3 (E) and the 2 (D). This is followed by the classic 1, 2, 3, 5 Coltrane idea. Next, the same phrase is played up a half step over the II V in D♭ major. Note how the phrase continues until its eventual resolution on C minor.

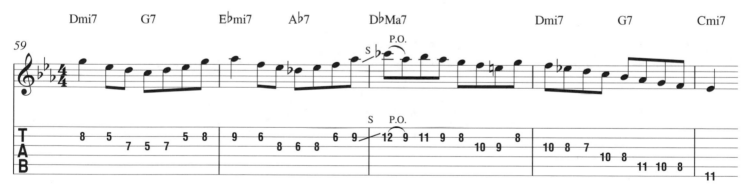

FIG. 11.1. "Moment's Notice" Measures 59–63

Measures 75–76 show diatonic descending 7 arpeggios in the key of E♭ major: E♭ major 7, F minor 7, G minor 7, and A♭ major 7 respectively. This modern approach is used by Mike in many of his solos.

FIG. 11.2. "Moment's Notice" Measures 75–76

Measures 97–101 illustrate the same idea as figure 11.1, measures 59–63. It is identical, with the exception of one note over the D♭ major chord (E instead of E♭ in the first idea) and the B♭ instead of a B natural in the first idea over the G7 chord. Pay close attention to how both ideas resolve on the 3 of the C minor chord (E♭). As a matter of fact, every time there is a C minor chord in this tune, Mike lands on an E♭.

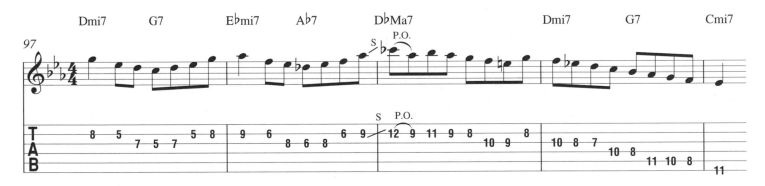

FIG. 11.3. "Moment's Notice" Measures 97–101

Moment's Notice
Solo by Mike Stern

By John Coltrane

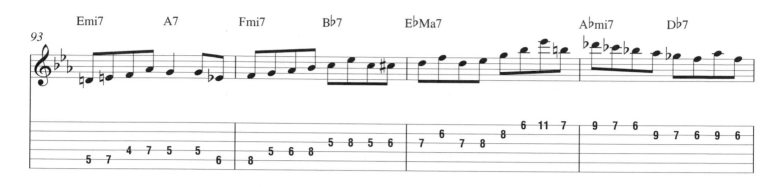

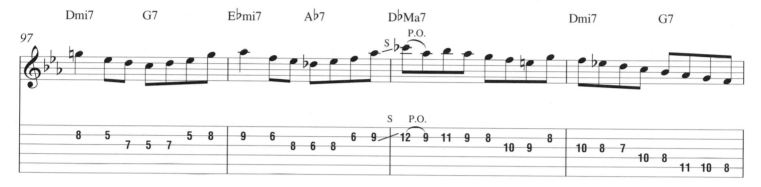

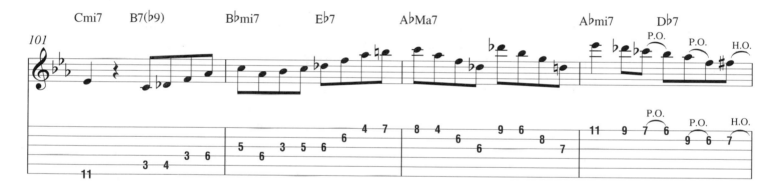

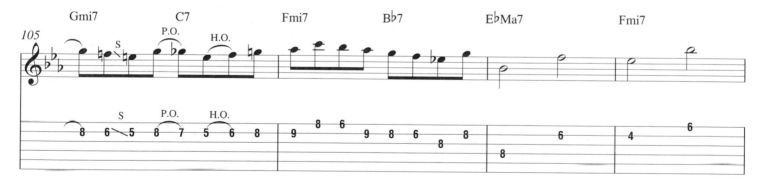

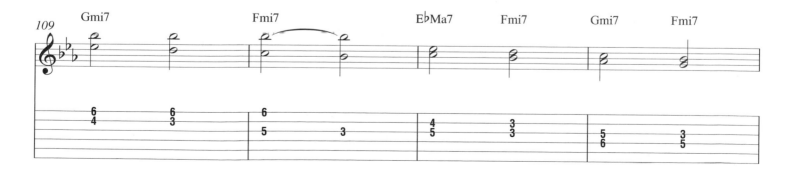

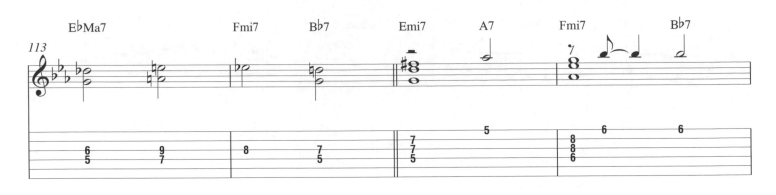

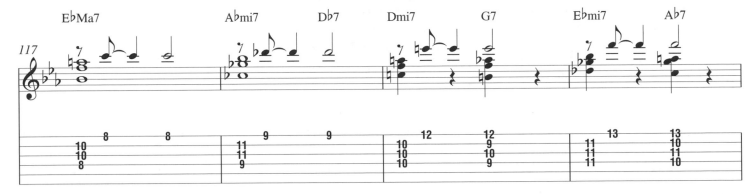

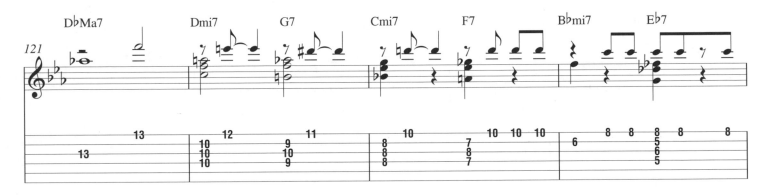

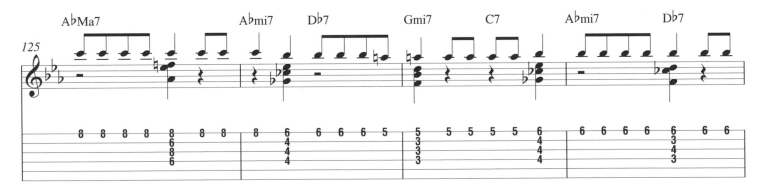

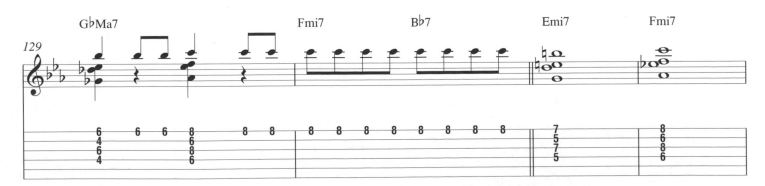

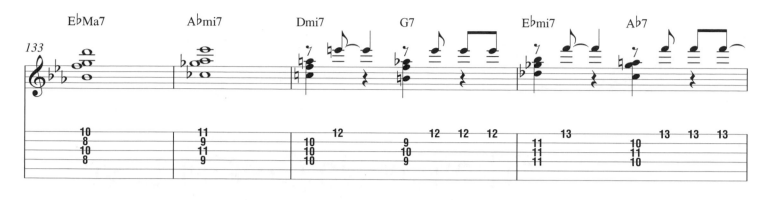

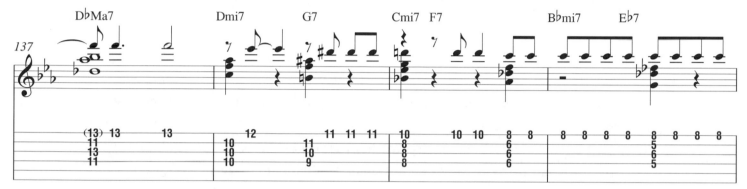

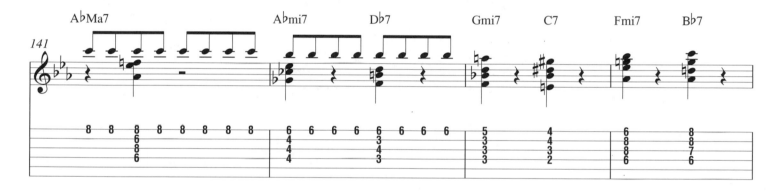

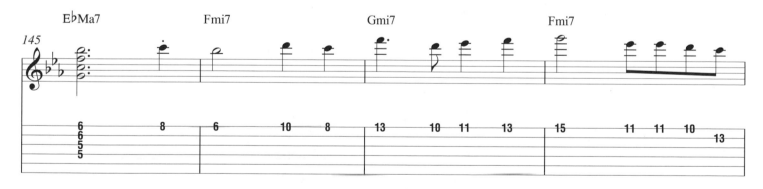

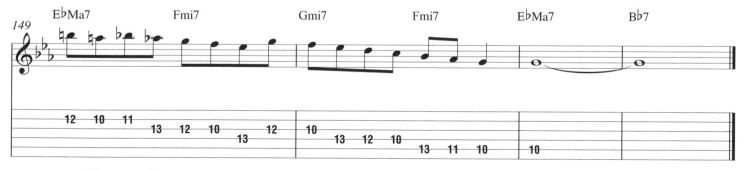

FIG. 11.4. "Moment's Notice"

"There Is No Greater Love"

"There Is No Greater Love" also comes from Mike Stern's *Standards (And Other Songs)* album. There were so many ideas in this solo that it was difficult to choose. Below are some examples.

Measures 12–13 show an E♭ dominant 7 arpeggio in root position followed by the 9, 11, and 13. Next, we see an A♭ Lydian dominant phrase (which is the fourth mode of E♭ melodic minor).

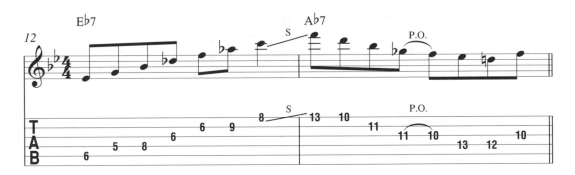

FIG. 12.1. "There Is No Greater Love" Measures 12–13

Measures 35–39 illustrate Mike's blues playing.

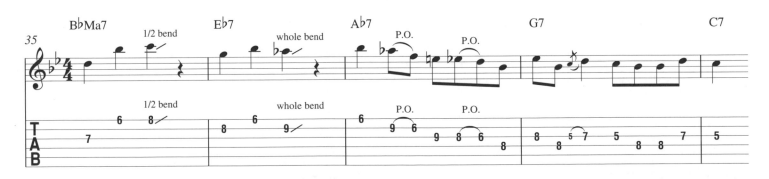

FIG. 12.2. "There Is No Greater Love" Measures 35–39

In measures 132–145, we see diminished 7 chord arpeggios going down in half steps, creating tension over the chord changes. This sequence of diminished 7 chords sounds very modern and again is indicative of Mike's playing.

FIG. 12.3. "There Is No Greater Love" Measures 132–145

Measures 200–210 feature a motif that Mike moves all over the fretboard. The interesting thing about it is that, because of where he places the motif on the fretboard, he gets different notes of each chord even though the intervals within the motif are the same. For example, over the B♭Ma7 chord in measure 203, he plays the 3, 13 (6), and the 9 (2), and over the E♭7 in measure 204, he plays a 9 (2), 5, and root. This changes for every chord while keeping the motif the same.

FIG. 12.4. "There Is No Greater Love" Measures 200–210

In measures 227–234, we see a variety of arpeggios, including minor 7, major triads, and augmented chords.

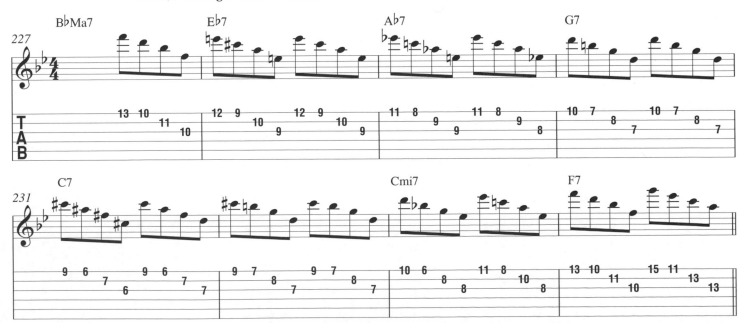

FIG. 12.5. "There Is No Greater Love" Measures 227–234

There Is No Greater Love
Solo by Mike Stern

Words by Marty Symes
Music by Isham Jones

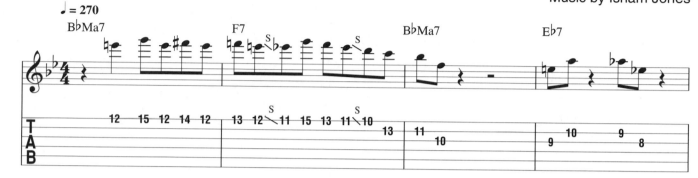

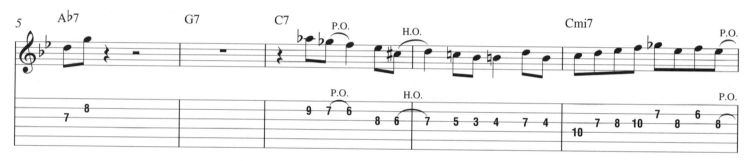

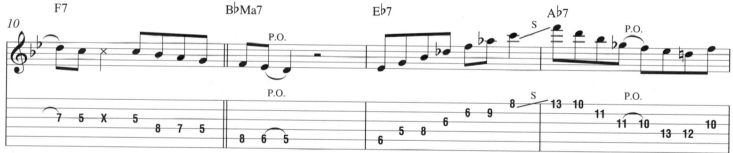

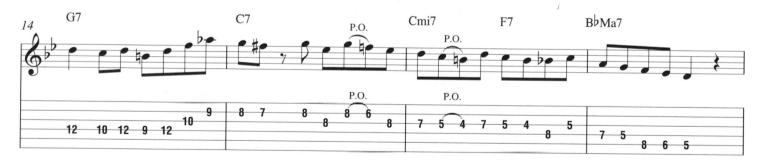

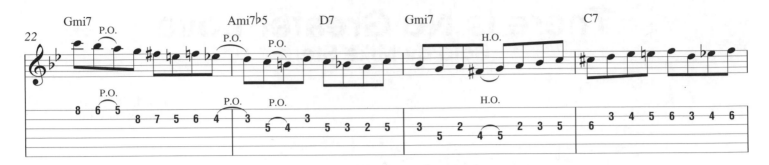

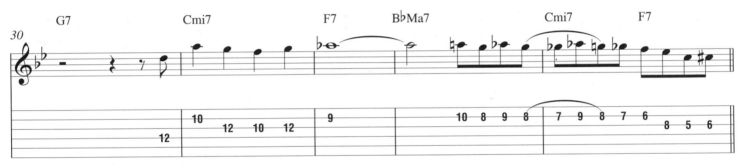

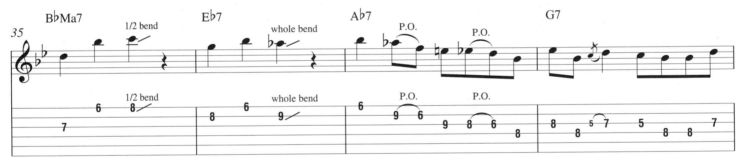

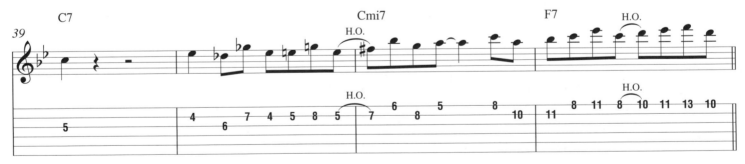

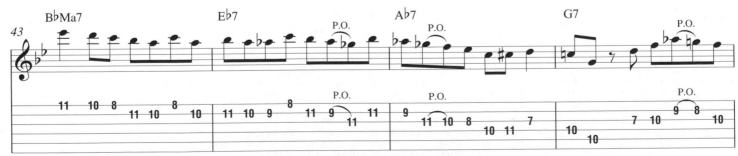

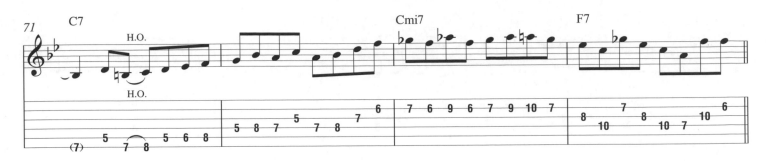

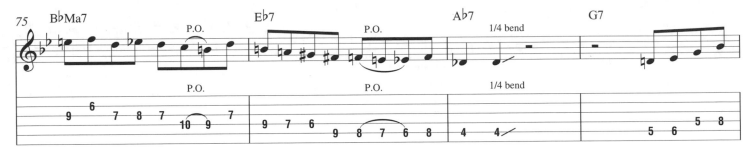

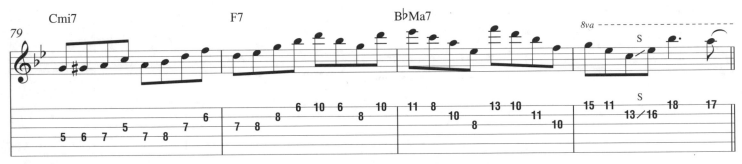

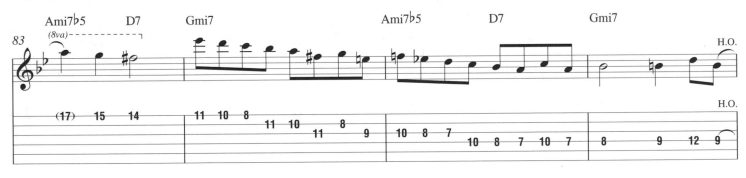

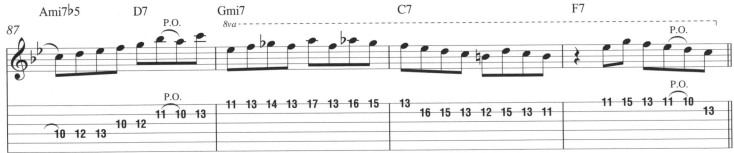

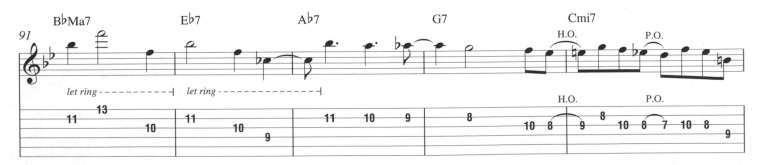

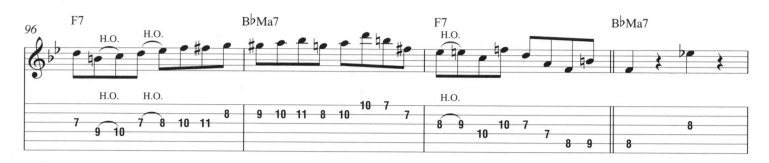

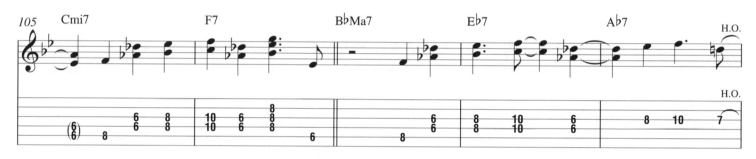

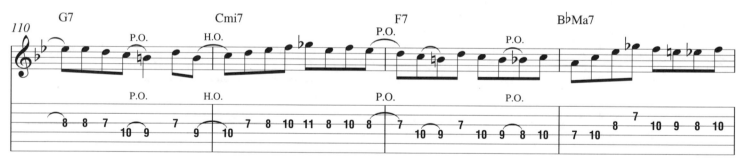

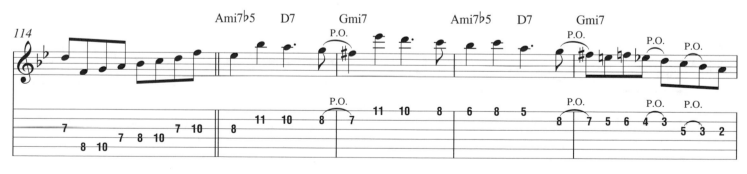

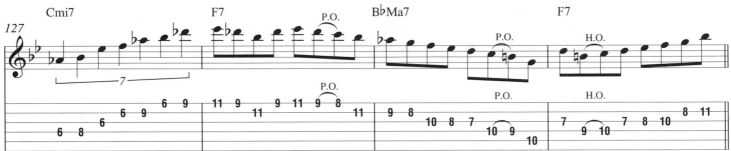

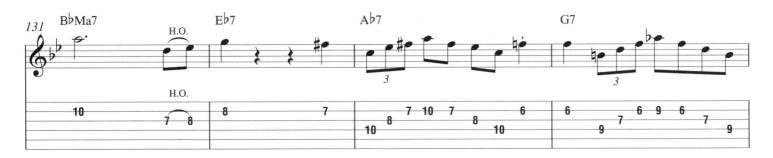

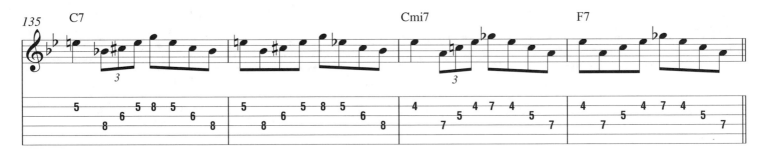

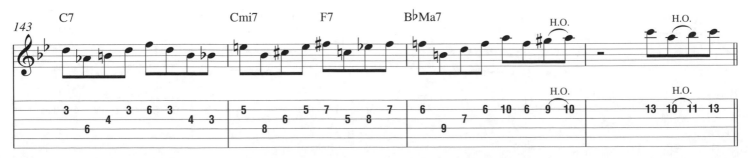

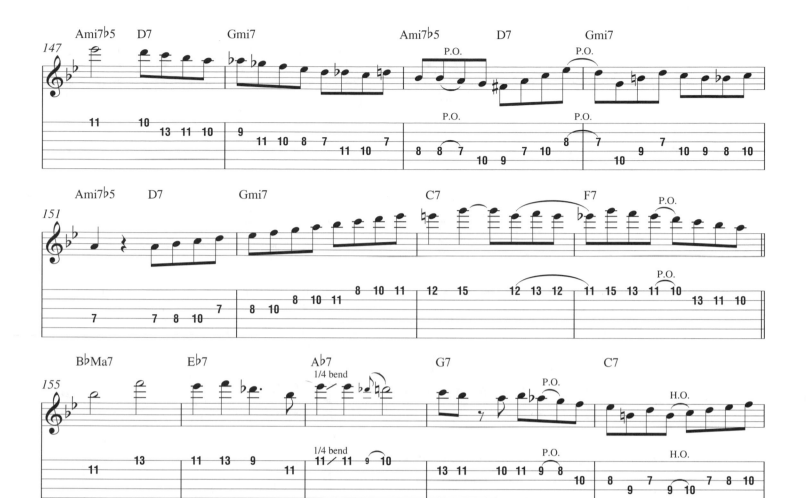

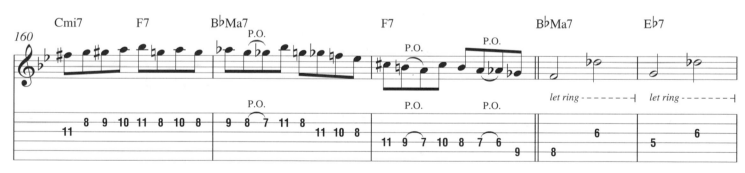

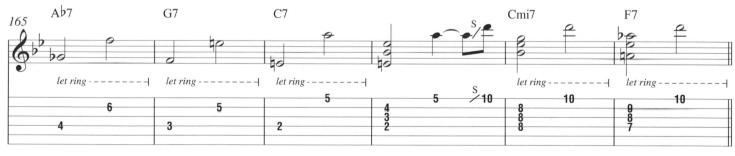

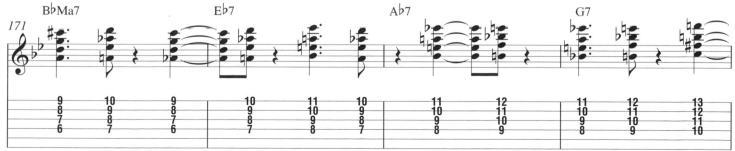

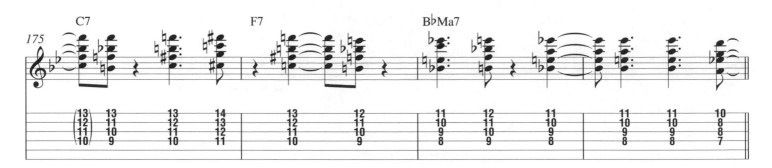

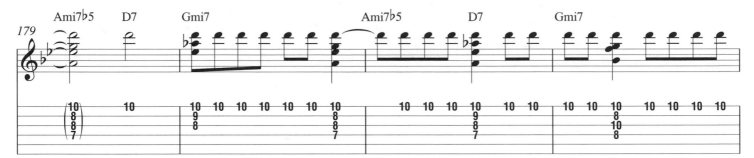

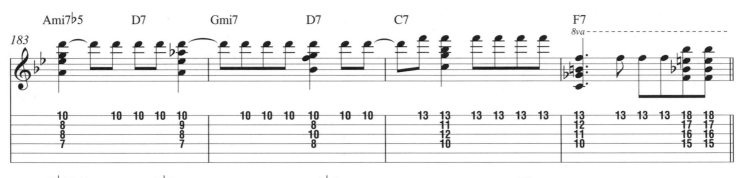

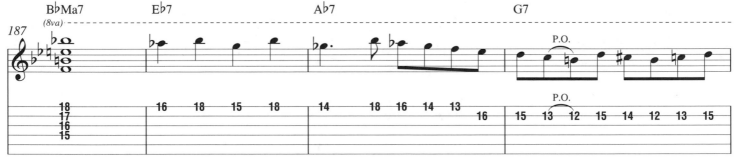

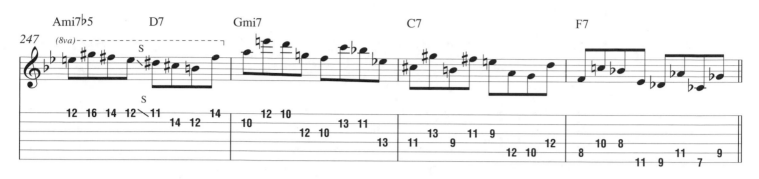

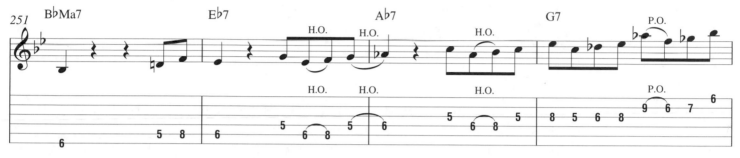

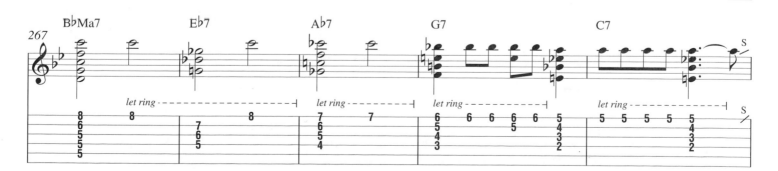

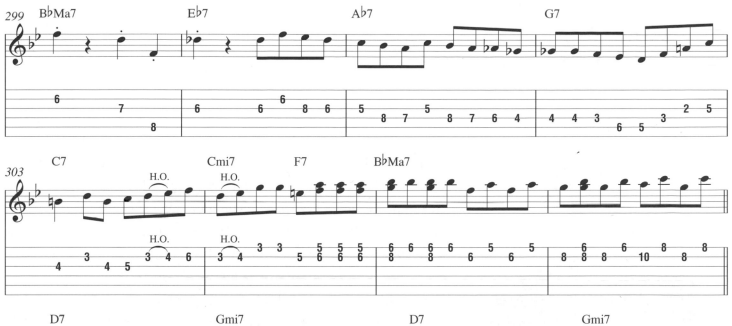

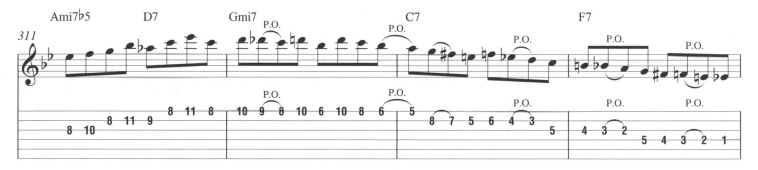

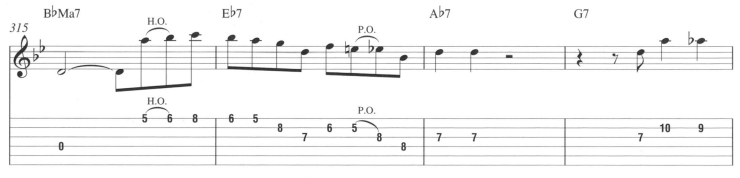

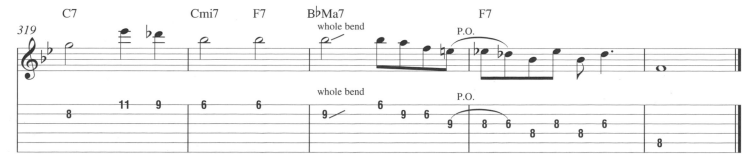

FIG. 12.6. "There Is No Greater Love"

ABOUT THE AUTHOR

Photo by 和田康弘 *(Yasuhiro Wada)*

Michael Kaplan is a versatile guitarist with a bachelor's degree in classical guitar and a master's degree in jazz. He has performed, taught, and recorded in almost every musical style. While attending the University of Miami, Michael had the opportunity to study with internationally acclaimed guitarist Juan Mercadal, who also trained world-renowned guitarists Steve Morse and Manuel Barrueco. Some of Michael's performing credits include playing with Dr. Lonnie Smith, Alfred "Pee Wee" Ellis, Rich Little, Dick Hyman, and sharing the stage with the Average White Band. He also had the honor of playing under the baton of Michael Kamen.

Michael has given guitar lessons and workshops in all styles. He was on the faculty of Nova Southeastern University, Florida Atlantic University, Barry University, Miami Dade College, and Broward College. In addition, he was artist in residence at the Kathmandu Jazz Conservatory in Kathmandu, Nepal, where he was head of the guitar and bass department. He has taught courses in jazz and pop history, music theory, chamber music, and improvisation, as well as conducted jazz guitar ensembles, classical guitar ensembles, and jazz combos.

In addition, he has transcribed and edited a play-along book on jazz guitar comping with Jamey Aebersold and Dr. Mike Di Liddo, and is the author of *Bebop Guitar Solos* (Berklee Press, 2014). Currently, Michael is the director of the American Guitar Academy in Tokyo.

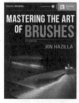